THE MILIT...
IN SCOTLAND

William Taylor

British Library Cataloguing in Publication Data
A catalogue record for this book is available from the British Library
ISBN 1-899863-08-7

Printed in Great Britain by SRP Ltd, Exeter
for House of Lochar, Isle of Colonsay, Argyll PA61 7YR

Contents

The Military Roads

Wade	Miles	Date
Fort William to Inverness	61	1725–7
		1732–3
Dunkeld to Inverness	102	1728–30
Crieff to Dalnacardoch	43	1730
Dalwhinnie to Fort Augustus	28	1731
Etteridge Cross Road	4	pre-1734
Caulfeild		
Stirling to Crieff	20	1741–2
Dumbarton to Inveraray	44	1744–50
Stirling to Fort William	93	1748–53
Coupar Angus to Fort George	100	1748–57
Tarbet to Crianlarich	16	1752–4
Dalmally to Bonawe	13	1752–4
Fort Augustus to Bernera	43	1755–63
Inveraray to Tyndrum	22	1757–61
*†Stonehaven to Fochabers by Aberdeen	84	1750s
Huntly to Portsoy	20	1750s
°Corgarff to Aberdeen	46	1750s
†Dunkeld to Amulree	9	1761
Contin to Poolewe	52	1761–3
*Fettercairn to Fochabers	66	1761
Bridge of Sark to Port Patrick	105	1760s
Coupar Angus to Dunkeld	15	1760s
Probably Caulfeild, but undated		
Grantown to Aviemore	16	
Sluggan Bridge to Dulnain Bridge	9	
Fort George to Inverness	16	
Grantown to Forres	13	
Post-Caulfeild		
Dulsie Bridge to Aviemore	20	1790s
Fort William to Glencoe	22	1786
Stranraer to Ballantrae	16	1780–2
Dumbarton to Stirling	34	1770–80
Perth to Perth Prison	(960yd)	1810

*18 miles in common between Huntly and Fochabers
†12 miles in common between Kintore and Aberdeen
°Mileage conjectural

Publisher's Note

We hope that the publication of this revised edition of William Taylor's thorough and well-documented book will be welcomed not only by the general reader but also by the ever growing numbers of people who enjoy tracing Scotland's history and culture by walking her hills and glens.

Since this book was first published in 1976 there have been surprisingly few changes to the military roads with the notable exception of the work on the new A9. Where specific details have changed the text has in almost all cases been altered accordingly, and particular thanks are due to Mr A.D. Anderson for his generous assistance in updating the details concerning the Dumfries and Galloway road (p168–70). However, for the section of the A9 between the Clunes Lodge area and Allt Coire Mhic Sithe (see p136–7), although there have been changes on the ground so that the military road has largely disappeared, we have left eh text describing the status quo before realignment and added some notes to point out the alterations, such as the moving of the Wade Stone (p137). Those wanting to see or to walk on the military road in this vicinity are strongly advised, in the interests of safety and comfort, to seek access whenever possible from the old A9 rather than from the modern 'race track'.

The Royal Commission on the Ancient and historical Monuments of Scotland are in possession of copies of a considerable amount of illustrative material such as slides, photographs and maps which Dr Taylor collected during the course of research for this book. This archive can be consulted by prior arrangement at the premises of the RCAHMS in Edinburgh.

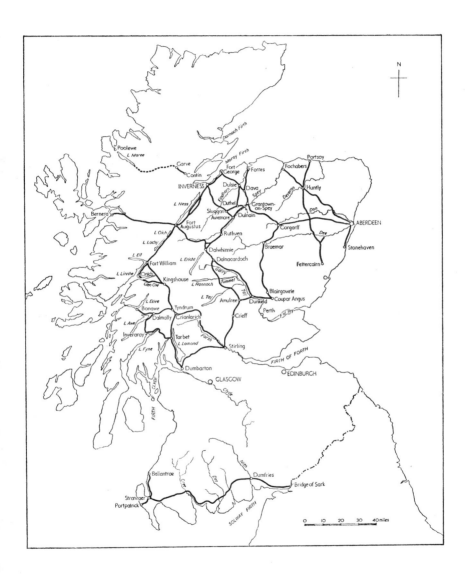

PART ONE

Historical Background, Origins and Development

Introduction

There has been a tendency in Scotland to attribute to the Romans or to General Wade any road or bridge of obvious antiquity. In either case the attribution is more than likely to be wrong. Such roads may not have produced a crop of Agricola's Arms or Hadrian's Howffs, but Wade cafés and petrol stations are not unknown. Although Major Caulfeild built many more miles of military road than General Wade, there is nowhere, despite the alliterative temptation, a Caulfeild café, probably because generations of journalists like Southey assumed that as Wade fathered the idea, he must have been responsible for the whole family of military roads.

In circumstances to be described later General Wade conceived the idea of military roads in the Highlands simply to facilitate the movement of troops and, with the exception of the Dumfries and Galloway road, all military roads were either in, bordering on, or leading to points of military importance in the Highlands. In 1732 Wade appointed as his Inspector of Roads William Caulfeild, and after the general left Scotland in 1740, Caulfeild was to be responsible for all military road building until his death in 1767.

From the seventeenth century the Commissioners of Supply for the counties had been given statutory powers to provide roads and bridges by levying a tax on landowners, and by using statute labour, requiring all tenants to give six days' work a year on the roads. Implementation of this obligation had been at best spasmodic, and to try to cut the cost of road works, most Commissioners used Rogue Money, a rate levied on landowners for maintaining imprisoned vagabonds. During the Wade era of road making Perthshire cooperated with the troops in road work. In the post-Wade era there was cooperation between several counties and the army. But when Colonel Skene, Inspector of Military Roads, seeking similar help, pointed out to Inverness county in 1774 that it was normal practice to provide horses and carts for repairing military roads, the reply was that statute labour was fully employed in repairing other roads in the county, and that it would be 'improper to work upon the Military Roads which in many Places lye at a great distance from the inhabitants'.[1]

A new road made for purely military purposes was a matter for the army, but to repair an already existing road was the responsibility of the Commissioners of Supply, and in the eighteenth century most counties received permission to commute statute labour for a money payment. So instead of having to rely on unwilling and unskilled labour, they could petition the General Officer Commanding for military assistance, and use the money to pay soldiers and craftsmen. Sometimes the soldiers were paid by the government, but usually the county was responsible. In 1749 the Earl of Rothes asked General Churchill for a sergeant and twelve men to instruct in road making in Fife, but as every available soldier was at work in the Highlands, Churchill had to refuse, thereby depriving Fife of a 'military road'.[2] In 1752 Sir James Carnegy made a successful request for help in repairing the road from Montrose to Bervie.[3] Troops were sent and paid at the usual rates by the county, so that this road seems to have as good a claim to be 'military' as other roads so described in the north-east. Another improbable candidate for military recognition is the old main road near Cockburnspath. Between 1780 and 1783, £1,500 appeared in military estimates 'to complete the Road called the Pass of Pease, being one of the great Military Communications between South and North Britain'.[4] An Act of 1789 allotted £1,000 from the Forfeited Estates Funds for building a bridge at Cockburnspath.[5]

The question may well be asked, 'what is a military road?' Is it a road made entirely from scratch by the army? Is it a road re-made and realigned by the army? Is it a road merely maintained by the army? Does it matter whether the soldiers are paid by the government or the county? In fact, roads in all these categories were called 'military' by eighteenth-century governments. It may well be that too close a definition would merely be an exercise in semantic pedantry.

It may seem an anomaly that the Highlands, which from earliest times had lacked communications, should be given the first planned road system, but the provision of these roads was neither a casual whim nor a charitable act by the London government. For centuries there had been virtually two Scotlands, the Lowlands and the Highlands. Over Lowland Scotland the king and his government had exercised control comparable with that enjoyed by their contemporaries in Western Europe, but in the Highlands there was another Scotland, where the language and culture bore no resemblance to that of the Lowlands, and which had been impervious to periodic attempts at assimilation. All too frequently control was exercised by 'letters of fire and sword', whereby a magnate was authorised by the king to act, with whatever barbarity he chose to employ, against an erring neighbour, 'with a prospect of reward from the spoils when vengeance had been taken'.[6]

How long this might have continued is a matter for conjecture, but the events of 1688–9, which forced the direct line of the House of Stewart, in the person of James VII, into exile was to prove for the Highlands a revolution in every sense of the word. When Viscount Dundee raised the Royal Standard on Dundee Law in the spring of 1689, active Jacobitism was born, and in launching the first Jacobite Rising he set in motion a train of events which were to have radical effects, far beyond their immediate objectives, on every aspect of Highland life. In an era of expanding industry and commerce, dominated by rationalism and materialism, it became increasingly evident that there was no place for the sentimental and emotional appeal of Jacobitism, which came to be regarded more and more as a romantic dream, inseparably linked with and entrenched in the far-flung northern Celtic fringe. As the movement persisted, it inexorably brought in its train the utter and brutal destruction of the life and culture which, paradoxically, it sought to preserve. Tacitus, describing Roman policy in the Highlands, put in the mouth of Galgacus the words, *solitudinem faciunt, pacem appellant* (they make a desert and they call it peace). This could have been applied with even greater truth to the *pax anglia* visited on the Highlands by Cumberland after the '45, when 'the Ten Commandments were suspended with the Habeas Corpus Act'.[7]

The Jacobites had failed to take advantage of the political turbulence associated with the Act of Union in 1707, and although there was a Rising after the death of Queen Anne, the leadership was weak, and 1715 was a year too late to make maximum impact. The government passed a Disarming Act which served mainly to provide many High-landers with a source of income from shipping useless arms from the Low Countries, handing them in, and collecting the fee for surrendered arms.[8] The estates of active Jacobites were forfeited to the crown, and more forts and barracks were planned for the Highlands, but the Highland Companies, formed after the 1689 Rising, were disbanded in 1717, because the government, with justification, felt that they were a waste of money. The Glenshiel affair of 1719, however, acted as a spur to fort building, and shortly afterwards forts or barracks were completed at Ruthven in Badenoch, Bernera, Inversnaid and Killi-chuimen (later Fort Augustus).

By the 1720s the Highlands were fraught with dangerous possibilities, and although over a quarter of a century was to elapse before there was another Rising, there was an ever-present undercurrent of unrest. But during that time a revolution of another kind was to take place. It was sparked off by a memorial, written in a fit of pique, by Simon Fraser, Lord Lovat, to George I in 1724. Prompted mainly by annoyance at the disbanding of his Highland Company, Lovat had no idea that his letter would have as its consequence the building of a network of military roads, making the whole region increasingly accessible to governmental control, with a dire sequel both for himself and for the Highlands.

CHAPTER 1

The Wade Era, 1724—1740

But for the memorial sent by Simon Fraser, Lord Lovat, to George I in 1724 concerning the state of the Highlands, it is probable that the future field-marshal, George Wade, would never have seen service in Scotland. 'The Highlands,' wrote Lovat, 'being . . . very mountainous and almost inaccessible to any but the inhabitants thereof . . . do remain to this day much less civilised than other parts of Scotland.' Having an axe to grind, he placed the blame for the unrest in the Highlands on the disbanding in 1717 of the Independent Companies formed after the Rising of 1689, 'composed of Highlanders and commanded by gentlemen of good affection and of credit in the country' (one of which gentlemen he had been). He asserted, with a certain amount of justice, that the Disarming Act after the Rising of 1715 had resulted in the clans which supported the government handing over their arms, while the Jacobite clans delivered up 'only such as were spoiled, and unfitt for service'. The barracks had no effect, because 'the regular troops were never used to such marches, with their arms and accutrements; were not able to pursue the Highlanders; their dress was a signal for robbers to avoid them; and the troops were strangers to the language'. There was truth in what Lovat wrote, but there was little evidence from the past to suggest that a local force in the Highlands would be actuated by a pure sense of justice.

There was sufficient substance in Lovat's allegations for the government to institute an enquiry. In July 1724 Major-General George Wade, Member of Parliament for Bath, and for the time being without a command, was sent to Scotland, 'narrowly to inspect the present situation of the Highlanders . . . to make strict enquiry into the last law for disarming the Highlanders . . . and how the Memorial by

Simon Lord Lovat, and his remarks thereon are founded on facts . . . and . . . to suggest to [his] Majesty such other remedies as may conduce to the good settlement of that part of the Kingdom'.

Wade set off immediately, conducted a thorough investigation, and his report of 10 December 1724 was a shrewd appreciation. He estimated that there were about 22,000 men able to bear arms in the Highlands, of whom about 10,000 were supporters of the government, but that 'most of the remaining 12,000 have been engaged in rebellions against your Majesty, and are ready . . . to rise in arms in favour of the Pretender'.[1] This estimate caused considerable alarm in London, and may explain the loosening of the purse-strings in favour of some of his later proposals. He confirmed Lovat's assertion that the 1716 Disarming Act operated to the advantage of the Jacobite clans, and that the receiving officials over-valued the arms handed in, most of which 'were broken and unfit for service; great quantities of broken and useless arms were brought from Holland and other foreign countries and delivered up at exorbitant prices'.

General Wade agreed that the Highland Companies had done a good job, but they had not been under martial law, and their commanders had been guilty of venality on a number of occasions. 'They are said to have defrauded the government by keeping not above half their numbers in constant pay, which . . . might be the reason why your Majesty caused them to be disbanded'. The barracks which had been built were grossly undermanned, and two, at least, badly sited. His concluding words were significant: 'The Highlands are still more impracticable, *from the want of roads and bridges*' (my italics). The most important of his immediate proposals were: the re-establishment of the Highland Companies, commanded by Highland officers and under martial law; the establishment of a fort at Inverness; a new fort for a battalion at Killichuimen, 'the most centrical part of the Highlands'; a small ship with oars and sails to be built on Loch Ness to carry 60–80 soldiers and provisions for the garrison at Killichuimen; and a new Disarming Act to be passed with more severe penalties.[2]

The government's reaction was quick and not unexpected. Wade was appointed Commander-in-Chief, North Britain, on 24 December 1724. In his proposals to the government in the spring of 1725 he pressed for a new Disarming Act, six Highland Companies, three of sixty men and three of thirty, armed and ready to join the regular troops at Inverness by 1 June. Two regiments would be required to garrison the forts and barracks in the Highlands, five companies to garrison Edinburgh and Leith. Of the six regiments of foot under command in Scotland, four battalions would be available, along with fifty dragoons to rendezvous with the Highland Companies at the first camp to be set up near Castle Brahan, where the Seaforth tenants would be the first summoned to surrender their arms. The troops would then move on to deal with the next clan, 'and so proceed from one to another as long as the season of the year will admit'. Money would be needed for building the boat on Loch Ness, for repairing Edinburgh and Fort William, and for building new forts at Killichuimen and Inverness. For this, for 'gratuities' to informers, expenses of camps, provisions, pay, and for '*mending the Roads between the Garrisons and Barracks, for the better Communication of his Majesty's Troops*', he estimated that he would require £10,000 a year for two years. The seed of an idea had been sown, but it is doubtful if Wade had yet visualised a complex of military roads in the Highlands.

The government, impressed by Wade's proposals, passed a new Disarming Act and empowered him to implement it, gave its blessing to his plans, enjoined him to give all legal assistance to Edmund Burt, 'appointed agent for the estates late of the Earl of Seaforth, and of Glenmoriston', and permitted him to 'defray charges . . . for repairing the roads between garrisons and barracks'.[3]

Armed with this very full authority, £1,000 for expenses of the previous year and £5,000 on account for the current year, Wade arrived in Scotland in the middle of June. Delayed by the Malt Tax riots in Glasgow, he sailed at last from Leith on 1 August, a very late date for his programme, if it was to be accomplished in good weather. After four days of contrary winds he landed in Angus and went overland to Inverness, arriving on 10 August. Probably this journey reinforced his resolve to do something about Highland communications.

The thoroughness of the preparations and the size of the force at Inverness impressed the clans. Fifty of Seaforth's chieftains came to make their peace, asking to be allowed to hand over their arms to regular troops and not to the Highland Companies. To this he tactfully agreed and fixed the date for 28 August at Castle Brahan. The solemnity with which this was done, and the seemingly abject submission of Seaforth's tenants, had an effect on the other clans beyond Wade's most sanguine expectations as he continued operations to the south and west of Inverness. Meanwhile the Highland Companies had been put through a course of training in camp by the regular soldiers before being posted for patrol duties. Despite the lateness of the season and 'snow falling in the mountains', Wade completed his task right down to Menteith and Dunbartonshire. He had collected 2,685 firearms. In assessing the success of the operation it should be remembered that he had estimated 12,000 disaffected men in the Highlands. It would be an exaggeration to assume that each of them possessed a firearm, but as only 2,685 weapons were handed in, there must have been a considerable number still unaccounted for. Perhaps the general should have instructed his men to search the thatch diligently.[4]

While all this was afoot, the *Highland Galley*, of about thirty tons burden, had been built on Loch Ness. Wade wrote to Pelham that it was capable of transporting sixty soldiers or twenty tons of provisions, and that 'she is seldom above three or four hours in her passage'. (In 1752 General Churchill reported that this extremely useful boat was in a sinking condition, with its timbers rotting away. He succeeded in reducing the repair bill to £100 by using local timber.)

The new forts planned for Inverness and Killichuimen had not yet been built, partly because of the dearth of stone-masons in the Highlands, and partly because of the 'excessive rains that fell during the whole summer season'. This probably explains why Wade had been able to carry out his entire operation for only £2,000.[5]

It was obvious that the government regarded Jacobitism as a real threat, to neutralise which General Wade was given a fairly free hand. It was equally obvious that the strong-points and troops lost much of their effect without good lines of communication and, for the first time in Highland history, resources were made available to a man with sufficient foresight and initiative to remedy the defect. There might be no masons to build forts; the summer might be wet and dreary; but men, albeit unskilled, were available, and General Wade was not one to keep them sitting in idleness. 'I presume also to acquaint your Majesty,' he wrote, *'that parties of regular troops have been constantly employed in making the roads of communication between Killihuimen and Fort William.'*

As a by-product of the government's anti-Jacobite policy the first military road was being built in the summer of 1725. The general ended his report by advising that 'a sum be provided annually for making the roads of communication; and a salary for the person employed as Inspector for carrying on so necessary work'.[6] The plan for a system of military roads in the Highlands was beginning to unfold.

In the following year, 1726, the various works went on, including the continuation of the Great Glen road up to Inverness, leaving only a few miles to be completed. On 7 March 1727 Wade's services had been recognised by his promotion to the rank of lieutenant-general. In the summer of 1726 he had written to Townshend: 'the Disarming Act has fully answered all that was proposed by it, and the Pretender's Interest is low'. Nevertheless the following summer he submitted documentary evidence supplied by his Intelligence service of 'some Transactions that were carrying on in the Highlands in favour of the Pretender'. Emissaries appear to have been sent to Scotland to see what clans would rise if Spanish forces were landed on the west coast before midsummer. As this information agreed with 'other Intelligence received from abroad relating to an intended Invasion in the west of England as in Scotland', it was taken seriously.[7] The garrisons of Edinburgh and Stirling castles were increased. The full Highland Companies were raised from 60 to 100, and the others from 30 to 60, giving a total of 555, at an annual cost of £9,140 17s.[8] The two regiments of dragoons and four battalions of foot remaining in Scotland were raised in strength, and a search was made for arms, but nothing was found except '25 rusty muskets in a cave'. Some arrests were made, and Wade assured the king that 'all proper means were used to frustrate Designs of the Jacobites'. Despite this, the principals in the plot escaped from Scotland.

This Jacobite flurry drew attention to the condition of most of the forts and castles. The walls of Edinburgh Castle were in such a state of dilapidation that, after the gates were shut, the soldiers could come and go as they pleased. The horrified Wade made four soldiers, fully accoutred, do just that, and reported to Townshend that 'they mounted into the castle in less than five minutes'.[9] £7,000 was made available in each of the years 1727 and 1728 for 'building and repairing barracks and fortifications in Scotland'. Fort William was to be strengthened and Fort Augustus was to be started the following year. This last was a major project and, though in use, it was still not completed when Wade relinquished his command in 1740. A final £700 in 1745 brought its total cost to nearly £25,000.[10]

The years 1728–30 saw the making of the road from Dunkeld to Inverness. In 1730 a road was made from Crieff to Dalnacardoch, connecting Stirling with Inverness, and in 1731 the cross road from Dalwhinnie to Fort Augustus was built over the Corrieyairack. In the following year, dissatisfied with the Great Glen road, Wade made extensive alterations in alignment. In addition, some bridges still had to be built. In 1734 a guard house and stable for thirty dragoons was built at Ruthven Barracks at a cost of £360 15s.[11]

In addition to all this, Wade had reconstituted the Highland Companies in 1725. In a letter to Lord Islay in 1731 Wade complained bitterly that as soon as they heard he had left Scotland at the end of summer, they went home and did not appear again until he returned! 'I am,' he wrote, 'under a necessity to put them under a better discipline or to free the Country from the charge of near £10,000 per ann. I assembled them at Ruthven to let them know I was no stranger to their ways . . . and that they must expect no favour if my orders were neglected for the future.' He seems to have reviewed the Highland Companies every year at Ruthven, and in this year, 1731, one of the commanders, Grant of Ballindalloch, tried to assuage the general's wrath. He wrote to his factor regarding three cows 'that are to be sent for the general's use. I want much to have the best sent.' The 'riot act' must have had the desired effect. It was reported in the *Caledonian Mercury* on 8 August 1732 that he had reviewed the Highland Companies at Ruthven, and had 'substantial reason to be well satisfied with them'. It was these Highland Companies, called the Black Watch by reason of their specially designed dark neutral tartan, which were, in 1739, formed into a regular regiment, the 43rd, later the 42nd Foot, with an establishment of 815, at an annual cost of £15,199.[12] It is a fitting tribute both to General Wade and to the regiment that the memorial commemorating its foundation stands at Aberfeldy within a few yards of Wade's most lasting monument, the Tay Bridge.

Lieutenant-General Wade had been commander in Scotland since 1725, and the government felt that the quietness of the Highlands was due in no small measure to his presence. It is not surprising, therefore, that in 1739 he was promoted general, and it was obvious that his days in Scotland were numbered. He was succeeded on 1 May 1740 by Lieutenant-General Clayton. Made a Privy Councillor in 1742, he was appointed field-marshal the following year. His subsequent experiences as commander-in-chief in the Low Countries and in England could scarcely be described as happy. His final appearance on the military scene was as president of the court martial on Sir John Cope, who was exonerated from all the charges laid against him in connection with his conduct of affairs before and during the battle of Prestonpans, a verdict for which the accused must have felt everlastingly grateful. Wade died at the age of seventy-five, leaving a fortune of more than £100,000, and was buried in Westminster Abbey.

Marshal Wade would have been the last to consider himself a military genius, and would probably have looked on his tour of duty in Scotland as his happiest and most successful. In a letter from Clifton to Lieutenant-Colonel Kennedy, he wrote, 'if the goodness of the Highland Roads and the convenience of the bridges has contributed to make your journey easy and pleasant, my ten years labour has not been in vain, as some would insinuate'.[13] The consensus of opinion is overwhelmingly in agreement that George Wade's labour on the Highland roads was, indeed, not in vain.

CHAPTER 2

The Caulfeild Era, 1740—1767

The departure of General Wade from Scotland in 1740 did not mean an end to road building. No new work had been done after the building of the High Bridge in 1736, but maintenance had been carried out every year by the Inspector of Roads, Major William Caulfeild. William Caulfeild was Irish, his father being a son of the first Viscount Charlemont. It is not clear whether he was with Wade from the start, but he was a subaltern in charge of a working party in 1732.[1] He must have impressed the general, because later in the same year he was promoted major and appointed Baggage Master and Inspector of Roads, a post which he held until his death in 1767. The experience which he gained under General Wade was invaluable, and later commanders-in-chief relied on his advice in all matters pertaining to roads. His advice was also sought by the counties. On 16 August 1743 Lord George Murray, chairman of the Commissioners of Supply for Perthshire, reported that he had consulted 'Major Cawfield' on the best line for a road from Perth to Loch Tay, and also from Perth through the Carse of Gowrie.[2] It is ironical that these two men, such close collaborators in road making, were shortly to be in opposing camps during the '45.

During the '45 Caulfeild was quartermaster to Sir John Cope. When it was over, in 1747, he was made Deputy Governor of Inverness Castle, from then onwards often being called Governor Caulfeild. He was also made a Justice of the Peace 'in all the counties where the Disarming Act takes place'.[3] Although he was promoted lieutenant-colonel in 1751, he was always known as 'major' or 'governor'. Just outside Inverness he built a house called Cradlehall which still exists. The name is said to originate from a device which he installed to help his guests. He was reputed to have entertained lavishly, to have been able to drink deeply without ill effects, and to have been able to outsit most of his guests during a convivial evening. As the casualties slid from their chairs, each in turn was carried to the hall, placed in a 'cradle', hoisted by block and tackle to the upper floor, and put comfortably to bed.

Caulfeild's respect for his former chief was reflected in the name of his eldest son—Wade Toby Caulfeild—names which still persist in the family. Whether or not William Caulfeild was the author of the couplet,

> If you had seen these roads before they were made,
> You would hold up your hands and bless General Wade,

it would be impossible to think of a better source.

Between General Wade's departure and the '45 the road between Stirling and Crieff was reconstructed, and a start was made to the road between Dumbarton and Inveraray. Progress on this latter road was rudely interrupted by the beginning of the long-awaited Jacobite Rising. Twenty years of Walpolian material prosperity had reduced to a minimum the possibility of support for Jacobitism in the Lowlands or in southern Britain. Nowadays it is obvious that Jacobitism was doomed as a political force long before 1745, but within the eighteenth-century context the time was well chosen. The Hanoverian government was embroiled in the War of the Austrian Succession, most of the first-line troops were furth of the country, and at that time, Prince Charles Edward had a fair measure of the charm and personality which characterised so many members of the House of Stewart. There, unfortunately for the Jacobite cause, the assets came to an end. With a French army, a French fleet and more French money, who knows? But with only the Seven Men of Moidart the outlook was bleak. The rallying of the 'loyal clans', welded into a military force by the genius of Lord George Murray, resulted in a combination of enthusiasm and efficiency which, allied with the ineptitude of Sir John Cope, resulted, after the victory of Prestonpans, in an Indian summer of brave but unrealisable hopes. The march on London was inevitable; the retreat from Derby predictable; and thrones are not won in retreat. With overwhelming forces returning from Europe, the choice was to fight the final battle in the suburbs of London, or to return to Scotland and hope for the impossible. During the retreat the victory at Falkirk showed that, given a reasonable chance, the Highland army was a force to be reckoned with, but in the event it was merely postponing the agony of the ultimate carnage on Culloden Moor in 1746. The cause was defeated and its adherents extirpated with Teutonic thoroughness. The butchery and brutality which followed the battle were unnecessary, but all too typical of those who ordered and condoned it.

The '45 cost the London government, in addition to any reputation it may have had for humanity, at least half a million pounds sterling, and to the government the latter was the more serious loss. While most of this money was designated as 'extra-ordinary expenses', two items are of particular interest. Cumberland, for whom 'Sweet William' and 'Conquering Hero' were incongruous soubriquets, accepted with greater avidity the government gratuity of 4,000 guineas. Prince Charles Edward, despite a price of £30,000 on his head and an expenditure of almost £15,000 on the secret service, escaped to France.[4]

At Culloden Cumberland had deployed an effective total of 8,811 men. Four days after the battle he was reinforced by a further four regiments. Scotland was divided into four districts, each under a general. Chains of military posts were strung out across the Highlands, and troops were quartered in every important town. On 1 September 1746 there were over 15,000 troops in Scotland, probably the largest military force since Bannockburn. The army of occupation remained at that strength until the Earl of Albemarle, made commander-in-chief by Cumberland, left for Flanders in March 1747, taking with him five regiments. Even so, when General Bland became commander-in-chief in August of that year, there remained nine regiments of foot, thirteen Highland Companies and two regiments of dragoons.[5]

It is probably true that, but for the resurgence of Jacobitism, military road building might have come to an end. The Dumbarton to Inveraray road had been left unfinished. However, the *Scots Magazine* of September 1746 reported that 'a small detachment of soldiers under Major Caulfeild are begun to work on the roads in Argyleshire'. This was the result of pressure from above. On 22 August the Duke of Newcastle had written to Albemarle, 'It having been reported to His

Majesty, That It would be extremely for his Service That the Road from Dumbarton to the Western Isles should be completed as soon as possible . . . That the soldiers may be employed in finishing the said Road.' Albemarle replied, 'We shall begin next week.' A fortnight later he was forced to report little progress because of bad weather.[6] In view of later correspondence between General Bland and Caulfeild there is no doubt that the report to the king was made by the Duke of Argyll. Work on the road continued in 1747, and plans were made, not only to complete it, but to start two new roads the following year, one from Stirling to Fort William, and the other from the as-yet-unbuilt Fort George at Ardersier to Blairgowrie.

There was no question of withdrawing the military presence after the '45. Jacobite estates had been forfeited, and their rents and profits were to be applied 'for the better civilising and improving the Highlands of Scotland, and preventing disorders there'.[7] Hereditary jurisdictions and military tenures were abolished; a more stringent Disarming Act was passed; tartan, the kilt and even bagpipes were proscribed.

> Much more than Jacobitism died at Culloden. Thereafter the disintegration of the old Highland society, already advanced in some quarters, was accelerated. The patriarchal authority of the chiefs and great territorial magnates was gradually transformed into landlordism. The demilitarisation of Highland life broke the ties of mutual interest and idealised kinship which had bound chiefs and clansmen and paved the way for a new social relationship in which the landlords came to regard their people solely as tenants and cottars.[8]

A War Office paper of 1748 detailed 'Posts to be occupied by the regular troops in the Highlands to put the laws in execution for disarming the Highlanders suppressing their dress and for preventing Depradations'. Highland forts and Lowland depots were to remain fully garrisoned and all the regiments of foot, apart from Guise's, stationed in Edinburgh and Stirling, would be 'employed in carrying on the new Roads'.[9]

The year 1749 saw a massive deployment of manpower in the Highlands. A War Office order detailed the 'Workmen to be furnished by the several corps in North Britain, 1749'. Barrel's regiment (King's Own Royal Lancaster Regiment) was 'to carry on the fortifications at Ardersier Point . . . [it] must encamp and must have at least two days in the week free from all work in order to exercise'. Barrel's were not to be allowed to forget that they were soldiers! No fewer than 1,350 men from five regiments were detailed for work on the roads, 300 from each of Guise's (the Warwicks), the Royal Welch Fusiliers, Pulteney's (Somersets) and Sackville's (Lancashire Fusiliers), and 150 from Ancrum's (South Wales Borders). An additional 80 were detailed from various regiments for the usual repair work. Herbert's (West Yorks), stationed at Fort William, was to provide 50 men to complete the fortifications at Fort Augustus. Three regiments of Dragoons, the 3rd, the King's Own and Lord Mark Ker's, were dispersed around the coast from Portsoy to Arbroath. In addition the regiments had to provide 15 officers and over 500 men for patrol duties in the Highlands. This duty was from June to November except for units stationed in the barracks of Ruthven, Braemar, Corgarff, Bernera, and Inversnaid, where they remained all winter. Even though housed within stone walls, the occupants complained bitterly of conditions. Inversnaid leaked like a sieve and the peats cut by the unskilled soldiery would not burn. In Braemar the fires smoked so much as to render the rooms almost uninhabitable. Official rations seemed to consist of little more than oatmeal, and it was not easy to supplement them with local supplies.

The effectiveness of this vast organisation must be doubted. Detachment commanders sent in monthly reports and often there was little to report. The soldiers seemed to spend their time lumbering after some Highlander still wearing the tartan, more often than not to be outstripped by his fleetness of foot. Cattle and goats were stolen from under the noses of the outposts. Perhaps, of course, even the soldiery had no stomach for the petty vindictiveness which succeeded the butchery. Whatever the reason, the Highland garrisons and patrols could hardly be described as one of the more successful ventures of Hanoverian policy.[10]

Meanwhile work went on apace in making the three major new roads, but the year ended unhappily for Major Caulfeild, who received what would be described in military circles as an outsized 'rocket' from General Bland in September:

I . . . have signed the warrant for £3,000. These roads grow so very expensive, that I have great reason to believe the Ministry will soon grow tired of them, Particularly the Inverara Road, which is of no other use to the Country but for the Ease of a certain great man, and was begun in Sir John Cope's time purely to pay his court there, and tho' you assured me that the Road would be finished by the beginning of August yet I now find it won't be all done this year.

The general was merely expressing what prudence had prevented others from saying openly, because it was obvious that the road would be very useful to the Duke of Argyll in his journeyings to the south.

So far the luckless Caulfeild had received nothing more than a reprimand for miscalculation, but worse was to follow:

The repairing parties may continue their work . . . tho' it should Exceed the Annual Allowance; Being thoroughly convinced that a quarter of that money was not laid out upon them the year before . . . from the Ruinous Condition I found them and where nothing had been done for three or four years, as all the people of the Country assured me . . . After such a demonstration, you must think me Extreamly weake and negligent of my duty to pass over this in silence . . . these Annual sums for Repairing the Roads, was not given you as a Perquisite . . . and you ought not to be Surpriz'd at my refusing to Sign your Certificate, for the Work done in the Summer of 1747; and which I am sure was not done, or so badly that there was no traces of it left.

You seem to think that you have not met with the same favour from me that you had from all those who Commanded before me. I don't know that I have done anything that could give you the least cause for Complaint, unless you expect that I should shut my eyes and say the Roads were in thorough good repair when the reverse is visible.

This was much more serious, being no less than a charge of peculation and incompetence. Caulfeild's reply, unfortunately not extant, must have been interesting, but it failed to satisfy the general, who returned to the attack:

Your former Letter said it wou'd be proper to break up the camps but not one word about what Working Parties you wou'd have left at each place . . . it can't be suppos'd that I can conjure such things of myself . . . Method must be strictly observ'd, or Blunders will happen . . . When you wanted money I cou'd then hear of you, but . . . you are quite unacquainted wth my Character, or you wou'd have been more punctual in several parts of your Duty.[11]

Once more there is no trace of Caulfeild's reply, but he must have made use of his Irish charm, because the general did certify that the work had been done and Caulfeild got the usual £500 for repairs.

Bland may have been determined to show that he would stand no nonsense, but he must have been influenced by the fact that the year's expenditure on the roads had reached a record £9,500. The affair emphasised that with the expansion of road works it was impossible for one man to supervise everything in detail. There followed the re-organisation which gave Caulfeild engineer assistants.[12] Caulfeild's relationship with Bland's successor, General Churchill, was cordial. He booked lodgings for him in Stirling 'where General Wade always quartered . . . my family offer their best respects to you and Miss Churchill'. When Bland returned to the command after Churchill's death, he was on much better terms with Caulfeild.[13]

During this time there are many references to a not irrelevant activity under the direction of Colonel David Watson, who until 1754 organised the military survey of Scotland between 1747 and 1755. Watson had been in charge of a road-building party after the '45, and had been acutely conscious of the disadvantages under which they laboured because of the lack of maps. He received five shillings a day plus incidental expenses, and he had two assistants, 'Stewart and Mr Roy who have 4s a day each'. Watson was a Scot and most of the survey of the Highlands was done for him by a fellow Scot, William Roy. Every year military parties were detailed for the survey, the NCOs and men being chosen for the qualities of 'carefulness and sobriety'. This valuable piece of cartography, covering the whole of Scotland, is the collection known as the 'Roy Maps'. They were never published as an atlas like those of Bleau and Speed in the seven-teenth century, but were extensively used at the start of the nine-teenth century by Aaron Arrowsmith in producing his maps of Scotland.[14]

Caulfeild, in his report for 1749, sketched future developments. A road twenty-two miles long from Inveraray to Tyndrum 'passing thro' an Inhabited Country may be finished in One year by 400 men', and a road from Fort Augustus to Bernera in one year by 600 men. This he hoped to do in 1750.[15] But things did not work out as he had planned. By 1750 the Dumbarton to Inveraray road was virtually complete, so work was concentrated on the Stirling to Fort William and Coupar Angus to Fort George roads, with well over 1,000 men employed. In 1751 the roads from Dalmally to Bonawe and from Tarbet to Crianlarich were started, followed in 1755 by the Fort Augustus to Bernera road. By 1758 work continued on the Bernera and Inveraray to Tyndrum roads. During the 1760s the Galloway road was made, and work was done on many minor roads in the Highlands. Since Wade's departure the work rate was not so great. Some of his successors were scarcely devoted 'Highwaymen', and it might have been better to have concentrated on one road at a time instead of doing two or three simultaneously.

In addition to new roads being made, regular maintenance went on, and there was increasing cooperation between the counties and the army, particularly in Banffshire, Aberdeenshire, the Galloway area and Perthshire.[16] In Galloway it was found less expensive to give the counties a maintenance grant than to send troops after the road had been made. County involvement made subsequent military withdrawal easier.

From the time of General Wade's departure until 1767, every mile of military road—between 800 and 900—was planned by Major Caulfeild, and his advice was freely given to local authorities planning their own roads. His roads were built at a cost of rather more than £130,000, with an additional £12,500 for maintenance. It has always been Caulfeild's misfortune to live under the shadow of the better-known General Wade, and even yet the name of Wade is applied to roads made long after his death. The fact of the matter is that Caulfeild built about three times as many roads as Wade had done, and while giving the general full credit as the originator of the whole concept, it is probably true to say that Caulfeild made a greater impact on the Scottish communication system than anyone before Telford.

CHAPTER 3

The Gentle Art of Road Making

When General Wade built the first military road in the Great Glen, there was no blueprint to which he could refer. He had to devise his own system. What ultimately evolved was something of a combined operation in which the basic labour force consisted of soldiers serving on garrison duty, with the addition of skilled craftsmen, such as civilian masons, and with an increasing degree of cooperation from the counties, especially during the Caulfeild era, not only in the cartage of materials, but also in the provision of civil labour to work alongside the military parties. The employment of civilian craftsmen on the skilled task of bridge building has often given rise to claims that certain roads were military because they had 'military-type' bridges. Such mistakes are natural because it was the same masons who built bridges for the army and for any landowner or local authority public-spirited enough to engage in road building or improvement.

Wade's military working parties consisted of 1 captain, 2 subalterns, 2 sergeants, 2 corporals, 1 drummer and 100 men, and one of his most remarkable achievements was to persuade the government to make an extra payment to every soldier engaged in road work. Privates were given an extra 6d per day, corporals 8d, sergeants 1s, and subalterns 2s 6d. For non-commissioned ranks the extra payment was the same as their daily rate, so that road work meant double pay. The road parties, according to Burt, were 'under the command of proper officers, who received two shillings and sixpence per diem, to defray their extraordinary expence in building hutts; making the necessary provision for their tables from distant parts'. If the weather was so inclement as to necessitate staying in the 'hutts', there was no extra payment for that day. Not being responsible for road work, captains had no special allowance. They had the powers of detachment commanders, and their task was to administer and preserve good order and military discipline.[1]

It was obvious that only the summer was suitable for road building. In Wade's time work began on 1 April and ended on the last day of October, but even within these limits there were days on which work could not be done. Usually about two-thirds of the work force started in April, to be joined on 1 July by a reinforcement, then both parties worked until the end of October. The number used by Wade on any one road was usually 500. This programme was considerably modified in Caulfeild's time, when the numbers were greatly increased, while the working stint was reduced to ninety days.[2]

The construction of a military road involved a great deal of forward planning. In the early days Wade had but little in the way of detailed cartographic material. In the course of the summer a survey was made of the ground to be covered the following year. Plans and sketch maps were prepared, paying particular attention to hazards which would require bridges and traverses. In the National Library there are several examples of these plans, all the more interesting because they were prepared by amateurs. After the appointment of four engineers in 1749 the plans and surveys proliferated, displaying an amazing accuracy and detail, particularly those drawn up by Gordon and Morrison in the Black Mount and Glenshee areas. It is a reasonable assumption that these surveys were carried out in the way used by Watson and Roy who were responsible for the military survey of Scotland between 1747 and 1755. 'Each surveying party under an engineer officer comprised an NCO and six soldiers: "One carried the Theodolite; Two measured with the Chain; Two for the fore and back Stations; the remaining one acted as Batman".'[3]

The detailing of working parties, the organisation of the commissariat and the collection of tools were matters of military routine. Before the main party went out, an advance party of a subaltern and 20–30 men met either Caulfeild or one of the engineers, to draw out the line of road, set up camp and erect blacksmiths' forges. In the Highlands the camps were either hutted or tented. In the south-west troops were billeted with the civilian population. The main party then handed in their weapons to the nearest military depot, in some cases as far south as Stirling, apart from a sergeant and sixteen men, armed with nine rounds of ammunition each. It must be obvious from these arrangements that after the '45 the government was quite convinced that there would be no real trouble in the Highlands. At the time of the Appin murder in 1752 there were over 1,000 troops within a few miles of the spot, fewer than 100 of whom were armed.

With each working party there was a small body of 'reserves', usually messengers and letter-bearers. The number varied from a lance-sergeant and ten men to a corporal and four men. The general realised that these men would be at a disadvantage, because by Cumberland's ruling they could get no extra pay, as they were not working on the road. All detachment commanders, therefore, were ordered to work a rota system whereby a different set of men were reserves each day. Sometimes the high command showed an amazing degree of humanity and understanding. It was also made clear to every commander that he could not employ more than his official number of men on road work on any day.[4] Correspondence on the Galloway road shows that the work rate expected by Caulfeild was $1\frac{1}{2}$yd per man per day, and Rickson felt that, by offering inducements, the rate could be stepped up. Unfortunately he did not record whether or not he was successful. He got 2yd per day without inducement, but gave the impression that he felt this could be bettered. The men seemed to work a ten-hour day, but it is difficult to believe that, as on the Galloway road, they always started at 3am.[5]

In addition to the military parties, civilian help had to be organised. Terms had to be agreed with masons, wallers, pavers, carpenters and blacksmiths who were required for bridges, traverses and cross-drains. Among Caulfeild's instructions in 1752 was permission to 'impress' carts. In 1756 General Bland required 'all Magistrates, Justices of the Peace, Constables' to help Caulfeild 'in providing Quarters, Impressing Horses and Carriages for forwarding Tools and Provisions . . . for carrying on the Intended Roads of Communication, and repairing those already made . . . he paying for the said Horses and carriages . . . Order to remain in force for 12 months'.[6] In the case of the more populous and wealthier counties, provision of transport for gravel and other materials was often at the expense of the Commissioners of Supply.

All arrangements having been made, the work started. While the military roads were the first to be scientifically planned, it should be remembered that they were designed for military use and not for civilian purposes. Wherever possible, and following Roman precedent, they were built in a straight line, going over rather than round high ground, though on occasion running alongside a river bank until a suitable fording or bridging point could be found. The width of the road, except in adverse circumstances, was sixteen feet, which in the eighteenth century must have seemed revolutionary, and which compares favourably with some Highland roads today. The tools were simple but effective. In 1726 Wade ordered from the storekeeper in Edinburgh Castle, 'Ninety 4 Shovells, 82 Pickaxes, forty-two Spades, 3 Iron Crows'.[7] To this might have been added screw jacks, wheelbarrows, sledgehammers, sways and gunpowder. On higher parts of the roads, marking stones were set up to help the traveller in winter. Some still remain, especially on the Drumochter road, notably the Wade Stone, a well-known landmark between Dalnacardoch and Dalnaspidal. The camps which were set up about every ten miles for the troops often developed into inns, or kingshouses as they were called, because they were on the king's highway. This impressed Telford. 'A very important Consideration also,' he wrote in 1802, 'is the erecting and maintaining of proper Inns upon the Roads. Several of the Houses which were built by the government upon the Military Roads are striking instances of the necessity there is of giving the People who are to keep the Inns something else to depend on besides what arises from supplying Travellers; there should be some land attached to the House.'[8]

Fortunately the raw material for road building was readily available. Stones of all sizes littered every potential routeway, and virtually every hillside was a gravel bank. In the early days the material was there and was used. Not until the nineteenth century did landowners begin to raise objections to road builders making free use of stones and gravel. First the foundations were dug. Then big stones, broken by gunpowder if necessary, were levered into the bottom of the trench. Smaller stones, smashed by sledgehammer, were packed in on top. Finally the 'coup carts' from the nearest hillside tipped on gravel to a depth of at least two feet, to be beaten in with shovels, wheels and human feet. In marshy ground the road had to be 'floated' on a raft of brushwood and timber.

The replacement of the gravel top surface was an almost yearly necessity in some areas, especially where the road clung to the rock by the side of a loch, and there was no space for a back drain. Man also played a part in the destruction of road surfaces. Not long after Wade left Scotland, Perthshire found it necessary to publish an order forbidding the hauling of deals or trees on the roads, as 'they were made for wheel carriages and were greatly deteriorated by such practices'.[9] In later years other counties had to issue similar warnings.

The earth which had been thrown up during excavation was formed into a bank on each side of the road, and the unmistakable shape of these banks today is a sure sign of a military road. Drainage trenches were dug on each side of the banks, and where the road clung to a hillside, the back drain was essential to keep the surface from being washed away. To take off the water to the lower slopes, open cross drains (Fig 1) were made diagonally across the road by the pavers. These cross drains were slightly sunk and paved with flat stones. It was not until the making of the Fort Augustus to Bernera road that mention

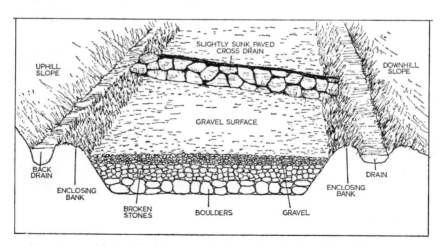

Fig 1 A cross drain. Until the use of culverts later in the eighteenth century, water was taken across the military roads by open-paved drains. This example is on the Devil's Staircase road half-way between Altnafeadh and Kinlochleven

was made of underground drains or culverts. Despite the cross drains, one of the major repairs every year was regravelling. With tar as a binding agent, the task of the road makers would have been so much easier. The first reference the writer has seen to 'asphalte' on Highland roads was that it should be tried as a surface for the Inverness bridge in 1857.[10]

When the ascent was too steep for a straight line, as on the Corrieyairack, the principle was to get the masons and pavers to construct well-drained traverses, zigzags or hairpins, supported by bulwarks of stone and mortar. Even today the walker appreciates the easing of the climb on the Corrieyairack, where there were originally no fewer than eighteen traverses, a considerable engineering feat. It may well be that if it had been possible to move from the eighteenth century directly to the motor-car age, more of the military roads might, with widening, have still been in use; but with the advent of the stage-coach in the nineteenth century, many military roads were too difficult for the horses.

While the soldiers were pressing on with the heavy, but comparatively simple work of road making, the masons and other craftsmen were building the necessary bridges or bulwarks and harling them against the weather. As all the bridges except the Tay Bridge were of rubble construction, this was a necessary protective precaution. There were always more soldiers than masons, resulting frequently in a time lag between road and bridge building. The final stage was the erecting of marking stones and milestones.

Despite the almost unbridgeable gap between commissioned and non-commissioned ranks in the eighteenth century, there was an unusual but natural *rapport* between General Wade and the soldiers building the roads. He called them affectionately his Highwaymen, and tried to ease their task by such things as ox-feasts and amateur brewing. It was also no mean accomplishment to have established that they should get double pay for road work. But all this is understandable. They were partners in a new and exciting enterprise. Wade conceived the plan and provided the means and the driving force, but without the soldiers wielding the pick and shovel, he would have got nowhere. No doubt the soldiers from time to time cursed Wade, the roads, the Highlands and everything connected with them; and from time to time the general was exasperated by the lack of progress, but they worked well together as a team, and they had very tangible results to show for their joint efforts.

Apart from the sheer physical task of road building, interesting social problems arose from time to time. In 1733 it appears that,

> In . . . the Highlands . . . their was no other drink for the soldiers than Brandy and Spirits; which rendered them incapable of performing their work, for remedy of which the officers did provide utensills and Stores for Brewing, and did supply them therewith. That the said officers are under prosecution in the Court of Exchequer in Scotland for the same and ordered to attend there the 23 inst. [Wade] prays for the said officers.

He also asked for a stay of execution. The dispute was not resolved because in September 1733 the excise officers were still 'surveying parties on the road when brewing and malting', so Wade ordered his troops not to give the usual help to excise officers in dealing with cases. In June 1734 Major Caulfeild and the other officers petitioned the Treasury about their prosecution. The dispute dragged on until June of the following year, when the Treasury issued a warrant to the Commissioners of Excise in Scotland to stay proceedings for the following reasons:

> The remote situation of the garrison, the unwholesomeness of the water, the spirits sold by the people of the country, the salt provisions, [all] render it necessary for their health to provide good and wholesome drink. It is necessary to brew beer because of the heavy land carriage.

The Treasury, pursuing the point, drew attention to the fact that 'ever since the Revolution all prosecutions for Excise of drink for the garrison have been discontinued'.[11] It is rather ironic that but for the newly made military roads, the excise officers would never have been able to smell out the illicit breweries in the hutted camps. Although conjectural, it is just possible that the troops might have preferred the local spirits to the ale produced by the amateur commissioned brewers.

Apart from General Wade, perhaps the greatest contemporary enthusiast for the military roads was Edmund Burt who described many aspects of them in his *Letters from the Highlands*. Burt wrote of Wade's roads, but there is nothing to suggest that Caulfeild used any more sophisticated methods. They all had at their disposal an army's greatest asset, its manpower. Troops were in the Highlands because of fear of Jacobitism, but there was a degree of enlightenment in using the soldiers on a useful project instead of drill and marching. Even more significant was the decision to give the road makers double pay, activated, perhaps, more by necessity than enlightenment!

In the midst of the great armed camp which was Scotland after the '45, Major Caulfeild had his hands full preparing for and supervising the road-building programme of the army of occupation, and from military warrants and letters some interesting facts emerge. Since the days of Wade's great adventure, procedure was more formalised. Paying of respects to senior ranks has always been part of the military code, and its rigid observation has always tended to diminish in direct proportion to the distance from headquarters. Being only too cognisant of this phenomenon, General Churchill issued a Standing Order in December 1751: 'As the non-Commissioned Officers and Soldiers . . . have been observed frequently not to pay a proper respect to the Officers of different Corps; It is order'd that for the future they put their hands to their Hats at least, whereever they meet Officers in the British service.'[12]

Much more important were the various issues of Standing Orders for troops working on the roads. One such order was issued by General Bland in May 1754:

1. No money is to be issued to any working party, more than their subsistence, till the said party has join'd the Regiment.
3. The Commanding Officer of each working party is to minute down the Days and Hours that his party or any man has not worked. [Weekly copy to the regiment and to Caulfeild]
5. The Commanding Officer of the party is to make a report every week of the number of yards of work which his party has done . . . [To be sent to Cumberland by way of the G.O.C. and War Office]
6. When any party has done working and has join'd the regiment the amount due to them . . . is to be paid by Major Caulfeild to the Major of the Regiment.
7. If any Person keeps a Sutlery [equivalent of the NAAFI] to a working party shall advance money to the men or allow them to run a debt to them, he shall not only lose the same, but be punished according to the Sentence of a Court Martial . . . to be read monthly.
8. The Captains have no Allowance . . . being sent to preserve good order and discipline.

9. [Cumberland] orders that no man shall be paid but such as were actually employ'd in working. [No pay for sickness, orderly work, or stoppage for bad weather]

10. Major Caulfeild is required to report to the General for H.R.H.'s information whither the Troops be Diligent or Neglectful in this Service.[13]

It may have been rather hard not to be paid for days spent on cookhouse fatigues, but it was probably wise to withhold road money until the troops returned to base, and to impose credit restrictions on the sutlers. Hangovers and efficiency are uneasy bedfellows.

The scale of equipment for soldiers working on the roads appears in a letter from General Bland in 1756. 'Each soldier on the Highland Service is allowed one Blanket, one Haversack, one Tin Flask and a reasonable proportion of Camp Kettles.' (The full equipment for a soldier admitted to Edinburgh Royal Infirmary is listed in Appendix C.) The army took cognisance of the fact that road work was hard on footwear. As Churchill's aide explained in a letter, 'the 6sh. is the price of a pair of Shoes and a pair of Stockings to each of the NCOs and Soldiers employed on the Highland Duty, and is allowed as an Extraordinary Gratuity'. Likewise the War Office was sensible on the issue of new clothing. Churchill was instructed in 1749 that 'new cloathing is not to be deliver'd . . . until all the working parties shall have finish'd their work for the Summer'.[14]

Immediately after the '45 troops were less comfortably provided for than in the time of General Wade. In the place of 'hutts' there were tents, thereby adding a new dimension of discomfort to the gentle art of road making. An entry of May 1755 could have appeared in any Order Book of the British Army up to, and including, the Second World War, so little had things changed. It was for 'Forty six Tents, with Poles Pins, Mallets and Hatchetts in proportion, with Forty Six Camp Kettles, and two Hundred and Twenty Five Tin Flasks for the use of three companies'.[15] It does appear, however, that there were huts in use on the Bernera road in 1756. In that year there were some officers new to Highland operations who kept sending complaints about conditions and equipment. To one of them General Bland replied: 'Get your Huts repair'd and turff [peat] cut . . . where Carpenters are unavoidably necessary . . . you have only to employ them and charge the Expence to me.' No one knew better than the general just

40

how many carpenters there were between Fort Augustus and Bernera. The most ingenuous request came from a Lieutenant Freake, on detachment on the island of Eigg, who asked, in all seriousness, for a coal boat to be sent. The general's reply was a model of ironic restraint. In a populous Lowland area the troops lodged with the local people. In Galloway, Major Rickson felt that this made for a more harmonious relationship between the soldiers and civilians.[16]

Food was always a problem even in General Wade's time, when he complained at the cost of having to transport biscuit and cheese. In 1732 this amounted to £66 18s 9d and Major Duroure's accounts show that 'There is a cask of cheese and a quantity of biscuit left at Fort Augustus, which Mr Caulfeild has not yet accounted for'. In Caulfeild's time the basic food was meal, provided by civilian contractors. Major Rickson made similar arrangements in Galloway. There was also a system whereby married soldiers were given an extra allowance of meal until such time as local provisions were more plentiful.[17] The lack of availability of local foodstuffs was one reason why road building tended to start later than in Wade's time. Early in 1754 General Bland explained to Caulfeild that he could not have his road parties until the end of June, because the year before there had been so little food in early summer that the troops did not have a 'proper spirit to carry on the Works'. The general was not, however, entirely altruistic. It transpired that he wanted to hold a parade at the beginning of June.[18]

It was finally realised in 1749 that it was impossible for Major Caulfeild to be present in person all the time at all the roads being made, so the War Office allowed him four engineers, and the following instruction:

He will give each [engineer] profiles of the said roads Specifying how deep the Ditch on each or either side should be and what depth the different layers of stones, Facines, Hurdles and gravel should be, as also what rise in the middle the Roads should have 1) in a Clay or Channely bottom 2) Along the slope of a mountain or hill 3) through marshy or boggy ground, and 4) through rocky ground, and also what breadth the said roads should have. He will likewise let them know what weight of Waters comes down through those places where bridges must be made, that they may see the same properly made to resist the torrents.

This was supposed to leave Caulfeild with more time for the 'vital' book-work which he loathed so much. Also, with engineers for the technical work, officers would have more time to see that the men worked 'chearfully and diligently . . . having an allowance for that purpose'.[19]

Fortified by the potential of the new system, Caulfeild submitted estimates for the forthcoming 1749 season before setting out on a tour of all the projects under his control, only to find on his return that his estimates had been queried by the Treasury. He wrote to Churchill in August, explaining that though the system was good, a new machine needed time to be run in. 'Tho' the Engineers are of very great use . . . they were this year strangers to the work, to the Towns from whence they were to be furnished with Coals, Iron . . . and by taking more pains to make finer roads than requisite, might prevent the workmen making the progress expected.' This was understandable.

The Treasury had taken exception to a charge of ten shillings a day for Caulfeild and five shillings for Cornet Campbell, his assistant. 'As to the ten shillings charged to myself,' he wrote, 'whatever additional toil and great expence I am put to in travelling over the Mountains and tracing roads thro' uninhabited countrys, while I am able to undergo it, I shall be content with what H.R.H. thinks proper.' As for Cornet Campbell, who had been 'at great pains and expence and has done good service. I shall acquaint him of H.R.H.'s pleasure and dismiss him.' He pointed out that he had cut expense to a minimum. Blowers, Pavers and Wallers had been cut to twopence a day and were complaining. Instead of carts he was using sledges driven by soldiers. 'I beg leave to assure you nothing would make me more happy than to have the Publick money put into other hands, but I have already used all my credit and if there is not enough money for the Masons and incident uses the whole will be greatly retarded.'[20]

In a subsequent letter he wrote, 'However concerned I am, and I am deeply so, to be thought extravagant of the publick money, it is a comfort for me to know that on the strictest enquiry I shall be found to act with the same economy which has hitherto gain'd me the friendship and repeated thanks of the generals under whom I served.' The main trouble was that Caulfeild was a man of action and not a bookkeeper. When he submitted revised figures in September, the Treasury dryly replied that it was £24 2s 3½d more than his first estimate.[21]

Despite his troubles in accountancy his bills for the year were paid. His working party consisted of 28 officers, 1,500 NCOs and men, 10 masons, 20 smiths, 24 carpenters, 33 pavers, 57 miners, 21 wallers, with 25 carts and 12 sleds, all at a cost of £5,064 19s 11d. Bridges cost £1,692 16s 7½d. Iron, steel nails and coals came to £100, and 'Paid to Mr Moyse at the factory at Leith and Mr Gray at the Iron Mills near Dalkeith £260'. The total was £7,117 16s 6½d. It would be comforting to think of the final ha'penny as an exasperated Caulfeild's Parthian shot![22]

General Wade had realised that roads did not last for ever, and that regular maintenance work was essential. Financially a distinction had to be made between construction and maintenance. In May 1733 Wade petitioned the Treasury for an annual grant of £400 for maintaining his roads and bridges. The requisite warrant was issued, and it should be remembered that Wade, as a Member of Parliament, was in a position to speak to any road business. The precedent having been established, the repair grant became an annual charge. In applying in 1739 for the grant to be increased to £500, Wade's certificate gave a good example of the kind of work carried out:

> The said W[m] Caulfeild did the last year Repair all the parts of the new road . . . from Crieff to Dalnacardoch and thence to Inverness, new gravelled the same and repaired the Breaches made by the violent rains. That he caused 9 stone Bridges to be new harled and repaired the Foundations of several others; and built large hutts in divers places where necessity required it, for the working partys . . . that he . . . employed 70 workmen beside Artificers, Carts, Horses, etc.[23]

With nothing to bind the top surface, regravelling was a recurrent necessity. Bridges battered by the winter spates required regular attention, and as most of them were of rubble construction, harling had to be renewed from time to time.

In later years 'maintenance' and 'realignment' became virtually synonymous. The best way to repair a road was often to straighten a difficult bend or level an over-steep slope. These matters were often dictated by the needs of an increasing volume of civilian carriage traffic, which influenced thinking at the end of the eighteenth century towards letting the military image run down and establishing in its place a new concept of Highland communications.

CHAPTER 4

The Wade Roads

If you had seen these roads before they were made,
You would hold up your hands and bless General Wade.

Fort William to Inverness (Great Glen Road)

In his report of January 1726 to the king, General Wade had stated
that 'parties of regular troops have been constantly employed in making
the roads of communication between Killichuimen and Fort William',
and so was born the first military road. Wade appointed Roger de
Bize Baggage Master and Inspector of Roads, and in 1726 work was
resumed. In a letter to Townshend from Fort Augustus on 16
September he wrote that he had ordered the road to be continued from
Fort Augustus to Inverness, 'so that before midsummer next there will
be a good coach road from that place to Fort William which before
was not passable on horseback in many places'. A week later he wrote
enthusiastically to Pelham in the same vein.

While still in London in April of the following year, Wade asked
for, and was given, a further contingency grant for carrying on the
roads.[1] In his memorial to the new king, George II, Wade gave a
progress report on his roads: 'The great Road of Communication
through the middle of the Highlands . . . is made practicable for the
March of Artillery or other Wheel Carriage, as may appear by my
having travelled [on it] in a Coach and Six Horses to the great Wonder
of the Inhabitants. This work was performed by your Maty's Troops
without any Assistance from the People of the Country.' So, by 1727
the first military road was complete. Bridge building seemed to lag
behind road making. In a letter to Pelham in 1728 Wade mentioned

that two stone bridges were being built on the road and that about another ten would be made the following year.[2]

The first military road had been undertaken with more enthusiasm than skill. Fortified by experience gained in other road works, Wade realised that the Great Glen road would have to be realigned, and in spring of 1732 he got a Treasury advance of £3,000, mostly for 'completion of the Fort William to Inverness road'. The original line from Fort Augustus to Inverness, on the high ground inland from Loch Ness, was difficult in winter and during inclement weather, so he planned to bring the road down to the Lochside from Dores to Foyers. This involved a lot of hard work and blasting, especially in the Black Rock area, where '2,000 yards [were] cut through solid rock'. Edmund Burt gave a picturesque account of the operation:

> The miners hung by ropes from the precipice over the water . . . to bore the stone, in order to blow away a necessary part from the face of it, and the rest was chiefly done by gunpowder . . . and where the precipices were likely to give horror or uneasiness to such as might pass over them in carriages . . . they are secured to the lakeside by walls.

As on other occasions Wade had spent more than anticipated. He had to ask for an extra £528 13s 2d, making a total for the year of £3,528 13s 2d.[3] He had actually finished with a little in hand, but had allocated £600 for assembling and preparing materials for building the Tay Bridge the following year. He had rebuilt and realigned forty miles of road and four bridges. One was the bridge at Inverfarigaig with a forty-foot arch built by the 'Dunkeld masons' at a cost of £150. A smaller bridge at Aberchalder cost £55. At the same time a sum of nearly £14 was paid to 'Mr Caulfeild for the General's Hutt', near Foyers, Wade's headquarters while supervising the road works.[4] The work was still not completed in 1732, but in the next year 184 men working from April until the end of October, at a cost of almost £1,000, were required to bring the road to the desired standard.

The most spectacular bridge on this road was not yet built. In 1735 Wade was authorised to build a 'rubble stone bridge of 3 Arches and 280 Feet in length over the river Speyer [Spean]' at an estimated cost of £1,087 6s 8d. The High Bridge, as it was called, finished in October 1736, put the final seal on the Great Glen road.[5]

Eighteenth-century travellers were impressed by the Great Glen road, both Pennant and Pococke expressing admiration for it.[6] Samuel Johnson in his *Journey to the Western Islands* in 1775 was surprisingly full of praise for the road, which he felt was good enough for a post-chaise, but regretted that it was impossible to hire horses beyond Inverness. The surface was so 'hard and level, that we had little care to hold the bridle'. The road was 'bordered by low trees, from which our guides gathered nuts, and would have had the appearance of an English lane, except that an English lane is almost always dirty'.[7] In 1763 a small detachment of the 21st Foot carried out 2,865yd of repair work, and between 1770 and 1784, when detailed accounts were kept, there was no government expenditure on the road, but £750 was spent on bridge repairs.[8]

In 1798 when military labour was no longer used, it appears from the accounts of Sir Charles Preston, Inspector of Military Roads, that over £112 was spent on road repairs and over £300 on the bridges. Between 1798 and 1813 complaints about constant flooding by the river at Inverlochy resulted in a realignment of 1,400yd by adopting and repairing 'an old road made at a remote time', presumably a reversion to the line of Wade's original road. Further alterations were made at this time at Black Rock, where there was 'one foot of ascent to every five feet of roadway'.[9] This road was handed over by Inverness county to the Commissioners for Highland Roads and Bridges under the terms of the Road Repair Act of 1814. In 1843 a 'handsome granite arch' was erected at Low Bridge to replace the military bridge, and two miles of approach road were realigned.[10] Shortly afterwards it became a toll road. By this time, although the military road was still usable, the main road had for many years been on the north-west side of Loch Ness.

Dunkeld to Inverness

There seems to be little doubt that, before finishing the Great Glen road, General Wade had a clear picture in his mind of future strategic road building. In any north–south communication system the key towns are Perth and Stirling, both of which should have easy access to Inverness, and he succeeded in persuading the government to implement his plans. In his memorial of 1727 General Wade told the king that if money were made available he would make a 'short and speedy Communication with the troops Quartered in the Low Country', between Inverness and Perth, which 'will prove the most effectual Means to continue [the Highlanders] in due Obedience to Your Maty's Government'.[11] In the event he felt that there was no need to extend the road farther south than Dunkeld. Permission was given for the road to be made and he was given a Treasury grant of £1,000.

On 20 July the general wrote to Henry Pelham from Blair Atholl that he was using 300 men on 'different parts of the road' and that he hoped to have made forty miles before October. The commissariat problem was acute, and Wade continued, 'there is so great a scarcity in this barren country that I am obliged to bring my biscuit, cheese, etc. from Edinburgh by land carriage which, though expensive, is of absolute necessity'. The fifteen miles completed at the time of writing were 'as practicable for wheel carriage as any in England'.[12] In 1728 the predicted forty miles were completed.

In 1729 General Wade arrived back in Scotland with an advance of £2,915.[13] Much of his time was spent in active supervision of the road works, with his headquarters in his 'Hutt at Dalnacardoch', where he received a letter from his friend, Duncan Forbes of Culloden, the Lord Advocate. 'Never,' Forbes wrote, 'was penitent banished into a more barren desart, to suffer for his sins, than what you have suffered in since your confinement to Drumochlter.' Obviously this was the year when the road was crossing Drumochter Summit. There was more than one possible line which Wade could have chosen, among them the Minigaig route from Calvine to Ruthven, an 'unofficial' road sometimes used as a short cut by the soldiers, but, despite later surveys, Wade's choice of Drumochter has persisted as the main route for both road and railway.

Wade wrote an interesting letter to Duncan Forbes in October 1729:

On the day after you left us at Ruthven, the Knight and I travelled in my Coach with great ease and pleasure to the feast of Oxen, which the Highway-men had prepared for us opposite to Loch Garry; where we found 4 [oxen] roasting at the same time. We dined in a tent pitched for that purpose; the Beef was excellent; and we had plenty of Bumpers, not forgetting your Lord[P] and Culloden; and after a three hour stay, took leave of our benefactors, and arrived at the Hutt before it was dark.[14]

According to the *Edinburgh Evening Courant* of 9 October 1729, 'they named the bridge where the parties met Oxbridge'. This memorable entertainment was a measure of the general's popularity with his men. Later in his letter Wade said that he had taken a 'second survey of the projected Road between Dalnacardoch and Crief, which is to be the work for next summer'. The hut at Dalnacardoch was later to develop into an inn or kingshouse at the junction of the road from Crieff and Stirling. 1729 had been a good year. Fifty-two miles had been made, leaving only ten more to do, which Wade estimated would 'require the work of 100 men for a month to perfect'. As usual, the Treasury grant did not cover all the expenses, and on 8 January 1730 Wade received a further £613 to make a total of £3,528 for the year. Wade's detailed account shows that for a two-month period there were 500 men working on the road. The cost of transporting provisions was £170. In 1730 the remaining ten miles were completed. This was Wade's longest road which drew the shrewd comment from Duncan Forbes that these 'new roads . . . must produce a Great Change upon the face as well as on the Politicks of this Country'.[15]

Although the general line of road has remained the same to the present day, there has been some significant realignment, notably from the straight line between Etteridge and Ruthven before crossing the Spey at Boat of Kingussie; from Kinveachy to Slochd by Sluggan Bridge; and from Moy to Inverness by Faillie Bridge and the Old Edinburgh Road.

The first major realignment took place in 1763 when a party of the 8th Foot, in addition to repair work, made 6,730yd of new road from Kirk of Kingussie to Etteridge, thus abandoning the long straight by way of Phoines. This realignment must have been traversed by Pennant during his tour in 1774. He was impressed by the road as a whole, describing Killiecrankie Pass as 'very fine [the road] formed by the soldiery lent by the government, who have sixpence a day from the country besides their pay'.[16] This is confirmed in the minutes of the Commissioners of Supply for Perthshire, where civil and military cooperation are emphasised, though the government bore the brunt of the cost. Between 1770 and 1784 the government spent nearly £8,000 on repairs to this road. In 1796 the road was divided into two sectors for maintenance: Inverness to Dalwhinnie plus the Corrieyairack, and Dalwhinnie to Dunkeld and Amulree.[17]

Telford's survey suggested an overdue improvement at the very start of the road in Dunkeld. He reported that the two ferries in Dunkeld belonged to the Duke of Atholl, who offered to pay half the cost of building a bridge if the government would pay the other half.[18] This was done and Telford himself was responsible for the magnificent bridge spanning the Tay at Dunkeld, and opened for traffic in 1808. Miss Grant of Rothiemurchus had always a great affection for the ferry at Dunkeld, perhaps because, 'old Niel Gow [was] sent for to play to us at the inn at Inver'.[19]

After discussions between the interested parties a major realignment was agreed between Moy and Inverness in 1805. The twelve-mile length of new road was finished in 1809, virtually the line of the present A9 by Daviot which, perhaps, may not be considered by modern travellers as much of an improvement on the older road.[20]

Between 1798 and 1813 there were other alterations. One of the most important was the realignment of over twelve miles involving nine new bridges between Carr Bridge and Dalmagarrie. This meant abandoning the road by Sluggan Bridge to Slochd. There was also a series of alterations between Pitmain and Aviemore of nearly eight miles and seven bridges. One bridge near Pitmain had been so bad that travellers 'preferred a dangerous ford'. Nearly a mile of alterations were carried out between Dalwhinnie and Drumochter, because on the flat the river regularly flooded the road. At Etteridge a further realignment of over half a mile was done to avoid slopes of 1:4 and 1:8 'blown up by snow in winter'. This involved building the two-arched bridge near Crubenmore Lodge. Alterations between Dunkeld and Moulinearn meant six new bridges and over three miles of road. Between 1808 and 1810 there was considerable correspondence on altering the line between Etteridge and Dalnacardoch. The idea was to rebuild the road at a lower level to try to avoid blocking by snow— but this disregarded the hazard of flooding by river. Despite strong support by the inspector, Colonel Anstruther, the change was not made.[21]

Miss Grant of Rothiemurchus, who travelled frequently on the road in the early years of the nineteenth century, made a number of interesting comments:

> We baited the horses at Moulinearn . . . a dreary, desolate solitary stone house, dirt without, smoke within, and little to be had in it but whisky . . . on through Killiecrankie, beautiful then as now, more beautiful, for no Perth traders had built villas on its sheltered banks . . . The old inn at Blair [now the factor's house] was high up on the hill, overlooking the park . . . a few miles of beauty, and then the dreary moor to Dalnacardoch, another lone house with a very miserable steading about it . . . nothing can exceed the dreariness of Drumochter, unrelieved by one single beauty of scenery, if we except a treeless lake with a shooting box beside it, and three or four fields near the little burn . . . further on rose Belleville [built by Macpherson of 'Ossian' fame], a great hospital-looking place protruding from young plantations . . . a new road has been engineered along the sides of Slochd Mòr, thought a wonder of skill when viewed beside the narrow precipitous pathway tracked out by General Wade.

As a final gesture, perhaps just a little improper for a lady of refinement, Miss Grant permitted herself to quote the advertisement for the stage-coach named the Duchess of Atholl plying between Dunkeld and Blair in 1815. 'The Duchess of Atholl starts from the "Duke's Arms" every morning at eight o'clock.'[22]

This road was handed over by Inverness under the Road Repair Act of 1814, and in 1815 the cost of maintenance to the county boundary at Dalwhinnie was £266. Perthshire had not implemented this Act, and the road between Dunkeld and Drumochter was frequently the subject of adverse criticism. The condition of the road was so bad that the northern counties seriously considered repairing it themselves, but as the estimate was £100 per mile, they did not proceed with the idea. Luckily good sense prevailed and the Perthshire Military Road Act of 1820 ensured that the road was kept in a good state of repair. By the following year it was a turnpike.[23]

In 1828 Inverness petitioned the Treasury to have the mail routed by Perth and Dunkeld which, they claimed, would take only thirteen hours instead of the twenty-seven hours taken via Perth and Aberdeen. They pointed out that a stage-coach ran between Perth and Inverness, and that all the inns had post horses. Their request was granted in 1836, when a mail coach ran directly between Perth and Inverness at a rate of $9\frac{1}{2}$ miles in the hour.[24]

At the time of writing, a major realignment programme has begun, some of the proposals either coinciding with or approximating to the line of the original Wade road. The new A9 will be on the right bank of the Tay, crossing the river about a mile north of Dunkeld House and following the military road for almost two miles, eventually re-joining the present A9 near Rotmell. North of Calvine the new road is between the present A9 and the Wade road, but between Dalna-cardoch and Edendon Bridge, and again at the Wade Stone, it coin-cides with the military road. From Crubenmore it will be on the right bank of the Truim and Spey, passing under the walls of Ruthven barracks, crossing the Spey north of Kingussie, virtually coinciding with the military road as far as Lynchat, and again between Aviemore and Avielochan. It will approach very near to the military line between Raigbeg and Dalmagarry, and again from Moy to Daviot.[25]

Stirling to Inverness

On 28 April 1730 General Wade was given an advance by the Treasury for 'a new road for wheel carriages from Crieff . . . [to] the river Garry of about 40 measured miles . . . to join the great road from Dunkeld to Inverness'.[26] The junction point was at Dalnacardoch between Blair Atholl and Dalwhinnie. The route was through the Sma' Glen and Glen Cochill to Aberfeldy, skirting the entrance to Glen Lyon at Coshieville, then to the western end of Loch Tummel, where it crossed the river by the finely executed Tummel Bridge. This bridge was built by a local laird, John Stewart of Canagan, under contract to General Wade, for £200, with a proviso that the builder must main-tain the bridge at his own expense for twenty years. Sometimes the name appears as Canagan Bridge, but by whatever name it is called, this delightful bridge was soundly built, and is still in use for light vehicles.[27] From Tummel Bridge the road climbed up by Bohespic before dropping down to Trinafour, crossing the Errochty by a bridge now open only to pedestrians, and past a former inn where Sir John Cope spent a night during his ill-fated 1745 campaign. Prince Charles Edward, on his retreat to Culloden, used this road, and is reputed to have reviewed his troops at the now demolished Ferntower House, near Crieff. From Trinafour the road climbed by a series of well-engineered traverses to the summit, after which the Garry had to be crossed by a substantial single-arch bridge before reaching Dalnacardoch. The expenditure for this year was £3,520 8s, which included the completion of the last ten miles of the Dunkeld–Inverness road.

The road was completed but there was a big gap to be filled—bridging the Tay at Aberfeldy. In 1732 Wade began to stockpile materials, ready to start in the spring of the following year. The bridge, designed by William Adam, who already had a considerable reputation, was described as a 'Free Stone Bridge of 5 Arches over the River Tay near 400 feet in length the middle arch 60 foot wide, the starlings of Oak and the Piers and Land Breasts founded on 1,200 piles shod with iron'. The building of the bridge was not without problems, as Wade himself reported:

> The Bridge of Tay . . . was a work of greater difficulty and also much more expensive than was Calculated . . . partly occasioned by the failure of a Free Stone Quarry and also . . . the Justices of Peace who . . . promised to furnish Carriages for Materials at the Country's expense, but did not perform it . . . The best Architect in Scotland was employed and Master Mason and Carpenters sent for from the northern Countys of England . . . These with some of the best masons of the Country and about 200 Artificers and Labourers from the Army were employed for near a whole year . . . The first Stone was laid on the 23rd April and the Work carried on a foot above the Pavement before the end of October, so that Wheel Carriages now pass over it. There remains only three foot of parapet wall and the Coping to complete the work.

At the beginning of October Wade wrote to Duncan Forbes from his headquarters at what is now the Weem Hotel that work had been slowed down by bad weather, but that he hoped to finish before his credit ran out. The Tay Bridge was by far the most expensive item on General Wade's road-building programme, costing £4,095 5s 10d, but he meant it to be good and it was good.[28] By any standard the building of this magnificent bridge in one season, apart from the parapet and coping, was a wonderful performance. Wade regarded it as something of a prestige symbol and as a lasting memorial, and in this he has not been disappointed.

In 1747 Major Caulfeild received £240 for repairing bridges at Aberfeldy and Amulree.[29] Between 1770 and 1784 the road and bridges were regularly maintained by military working parties at a cost of nearly £2,500, including repairs to the Tay Bridge which, in 1774, was 'in great danger'.[30] The road was also in the comprehensive list of 1796 when repairs cost over £114. Just after this about 1,000yd of alteration was made at Coshieville, 'to avoid a very dangerous steep and almost impassable tract of road'. As Perthshire had not implemented the 1814 Road Repair Act, it must be assumed that this road suffered the same neglect as the other military roads in the county. However, the Commissioners for Highland Roads and Bridges recorded that the Duke of Atholl 'and others have recently repaired the . . . Crieff—Dalnacardoch road for £17,000'.[31] It is likely that this was when the various realignments were carried out in the Sma' Glen, and from Amulree, on the opposite side of Glen Cochill.

Once the road had been made between Crieff and Dalnacardoch, it was logical to improve the line to Stirling, and after Wade left Scotland, this was the first road undertaken by Major Caulfeild on his own. General Clayton, Wade's successor, writing to the Treasury, claimed that 'the Grand Entrance to the North Highlands is from the town of Stirling, from which place to the village of Crieff . . . the road is in so bad a condition as to be in a manner impassable, and should there be occasion to march troops or carry artillery it would be impossible to do either'. He estimated the cost at £941 2s, and a warrant was issued.[32]

Much of the work was reconstruction and realignment. In 1741 the Commissioners of Supply for Perthshire received a 'Petition by Major William Cawfeild . . . that . . . making a King's High Road betwixt Ardoch and Crief he was under a necessity in order to make the road straight and more Commodious to carry the same through a small Shade of Corns . . . The value thereof amounting to three pounds fourteen shillings and sixpence half penny Sterling was paid to the private parties'.[33] The commissioners agreed to pay. This is the only example which has come to light, apart from an oblique reference in the Stirlingshire minutes, of compensation being paid by the military road builders. It was, of course, in the Lowlands. Farther north the roads hardly ever impinged on arable land. In the spring of 1742 General Clayton received a further £218 for completion of the road.[34] The most expensive single item, the bridge over the Allan, cost £150.

On 7 May 1745 the commissioners noted, with some anxiety, that the bridge at Ardoch was level with the water and in some need of repair. An appeal for help was quickly answered. On 13 May, the last meeting of the commissioners until 4 March 1746, and the last over which Lord George Murray presided, it was noted that Caulfeild had sent fifty men 'to mend the new road betwixt the Bridge of Ardoch and Dunblane' and asked for local labour to carry gravel. This was done. In 1750 the commissioners noted that in response to several complaints about 'the steep ascent of the Bridge of Allan near Ardoch', Major Caulfeild proposed to take the bridge down and rebuild it, if the county would provide men and materials. In 1751 the bridge was rebuilt for £35 17s 8¾d sterling.[35]

This road thereafter was always regarded as military, even at the end of the century, and was an interesting example of cooperation between the military and civil authorities. Thus by the end of 1742 Stirling was connected to Inverness and Fort Augustus by military road all the way.

Dalwhinnie to Fort Augustus

By 1730 there was a road joining the forts in the Great Glen, and roads from Inverness to Perth and Stirling, but there was still no road from the central Highlands to the Great Glen. At the head of Drumochter Pass the distance from Dalwhinnie to Fort Augustus was only twenty-eight miles. The disadvantage, which might have deterred a civilian engineer, was that the road would have to climb to a height of 2,500ft. But having satisfied himself that the difficulties were not, from a military point of view, insuperable, General Wade decided that the programme for 1731 would be a road from Dalwhinnie by the headwaters of the Spey and the Corrieyairack Pass to Fort Augustus.

In the spring of 1731 Wade received his usual £3,000 for road building and once more at the end of the season had to claim a supplementary grant, this time of £281 4s 8d. He employed 348 men from April until October, and a further 162 from July onwards, giving a total of over 500. The crossing of the Spey forced him to build his first double-arched bridge at Garbhamòr, just by the camp which was later to become a kingshouse. This bridge, 180ft long, with two 45ft arches, was not completed until 1732. Its cost, and that of another four single-arch bridges, was £466.[36] The ascent of the Corrieyairack required eighteen traverses, which was no mean feat of engineering.

In a letter to Lord Islay in October Wade complained that six weeks of almost continual rain had held him up, 'but I still hope in a fortnight to pass the Coriarick Mountain in my coach'.[37] His hopes were justified. The road was finished by the end of October. To have built a road across the Corrieyairack in such conditions was a fine accomplishment, which merited the reward from the general to his men described thus by an eye-witness:

> Upon entering into a little glen among the hills called Laggan a Vannah, but now by the soldiers Snugburgh, I heard the noise of many people, and saw six great fires, about each of which a number of soldiers were very busy . . . An officer invited me to drink their majestie's healths. I attended him to each fire, and found these were the six working parties of Tattons, Montagues, Mark Kers, and Handysides regiments, and the party from the Highland Companies . . . who had this summer . . . completed the great road for wheel-carriages between Fort Augustus and Ruthven. It being the 30th October, his Majesty's birthday, General Wade had given to each detachment an ox-feast, and liquor; six oxen were roasted whole, one at the head of each party. The joy was great, both upon the occasion of the day, and the work's being completed, which is really a wonderful undertaking.[38]

It is typical of Wade that, having enjoyed his ox-feast at Oxbridge, above Dalnaspidal, he organised another such festivity to commemorate what was his most difficult accomplishment, though the general might not have gone so far as the enthusiast, Edmund Burt, who claimed that the Corrieyairack 'is rendered everywhere more easy for Wheel Carriages than Highgate Hill'.[39]

Wade sent a detailed statement of his work and accounts to the Treasury, showing that the road had been made by seven officers and 510 men; that the road was '28 Measured Miles in length', and 'made through a part of the Country that was scarcely passable for Man or Horse, being carried over the Coriarick Mountain (one of the highest in the Highlands) . . . and is now made as easy and practicable for Wheel Carriage as any road in the Country . . .' The pay of the NCOs, soldiers and thirty 'artificers' came to £2,044 14s 8d. The 'Incident Charges' were as follows:

Commission Officers for attention on Work	£170
10 Carthorses, harness, repairing carts and forges	£120

Tools, Timber and Sea coal for travelling forges	£ 80
Carriage of 6 months provisions and stores	£130
Forrage, building hutts, Firing and Medicine	£120
Poundage on £3,000 Advanced on Acct.	£150

The bridges cost £466, and the total was £3,281 4s 9d.[40]

The Corrieyairack was maintained as a military road during the eighteenth century, and in 1763 there is reference to repairs being carried out by a detachment of the Royal Scots Fusiliers over a distance of 1,700yd. From 1770 to 1784 there was no record of expenditure on the road, but a modest £332 was spent on the bridges.[41] The Corrieyairack road was handed over by Inverness to the Commissioners for Highland Roads and Bridges under the terms of the 1814 Road Repair Act. Unfortunately the making of the Laggan road, at the 'appalling cost' of £23,000, made the Corrieyairack road something of a redundancy in the eyes of the commissioners. They decided that it would no longer be repaired after 1830 apart from the eight miles between Dalwhinnie and the junction with the Laggan road. In 1828, Joseph Mitchell, the road inspector, reported to the commissioners that the northern part of the road had been abandoned for a year and would be superseded by the Laggan road, but that the bridges would be maintained 'on account of their occasional accommodation as a passage for cattle'.[42] They were still being repaired in 1850. So the Corrieyairack became once more virtually a drove road, and the writer, a few years ago, talked to an old man in Lochaber who, as a boy, had taken cattle over the Corrieyairack on many occasions.

From some points of view it can be regarded as a tragedy that this spectacular route is no longer open to traffic, because it would have been a wonderful tourist asset. On the other hand, those who are still sound in wind and limb must be thankful that they can still enjoy the Corrieyairack, free from the roar of traffic and the pollution of exhaust fumes. To the soldiers who built it, it was just another, if rather more difficult, task accomplished, but even in ruin it remains a wonderful memorial to their skill and ingenuity.

'Completing the Mileage'

General Wade frequently claimed that he made 250 miles of road in the

Highlands, and there appears to be no reason to doubt him. The Great Glen road was 60 miles; Dunkeld to Inverness was 102 miles; Crieff to Dalnacardoch was 43 miles; Dalwhinnie to Fort Augustus was 28 miles. This adds up to 233, leaving 17 miles to be accounted for. The ten-mile stretch of new road from Dores to Foyers leaves seven or eight miles to place. In 1732 General Wade intimated that he had a further ten miles to make on the Great Glen road, yet in 1733 he certified that twenty miles were built, but without indication as to where they were. Without documentary proof it is impossible to come to a definite conclusion about the extra mileage, but some of it could refer to the link road between Ruthven Barracks and the Corrieyairack at Cat-lodge. This road was in existence in 1735, because in January of that year Wade described the barracks as being 'where three of the roads lately made through the said Highlands do meet'.[43] Obviously he meant the road from Inverness to Ruthven, and its continuation south to Perth and Stirling.

The third road can refer only to one leading westwards, because the projected road to Braemar was never made. In April of the same year he certified that Major Caulfeild had 'repaired the cross road from Garramoore, [Garbhamòr] to Ruthven'.[44] The military need for such a road is obvious and if it had not been made, it would not have been repaired. In the north-east or the Lowlands, it could well have been a civilian road, but in the centre of the Highlands, in the mid-1730s, it could only have been made by General Wade. Coming from the south, the Corrieyairack road branched off at Dalwhinnie to Catlodge, but there has been controversy on the location of the connecting road from Ruthven. The logic of military necessity favours such a link; the difference of opinion is entirely concerned with the actual line taken.

Of the maps made at the time of the '45, Rutherford shows no road at all. Cooper shows a direct road from Ruthven to Catlodge, crossing the Spey, but Cooper was scarcely the most accurate of cartographers, showing, for instance, the Minigaig as a military road. Willdey shows a road from Etteridge to Catlodge, a line also shown by Roy in the 1750s. Roy shows no direct road from the barracks to Catlodge. The name Ruthven appears in relation to this road, but it should be remembered that this name often refers to the district, and not necessarily to the barracks as such, and a 'road from Ruthven to Garbhamòr' does

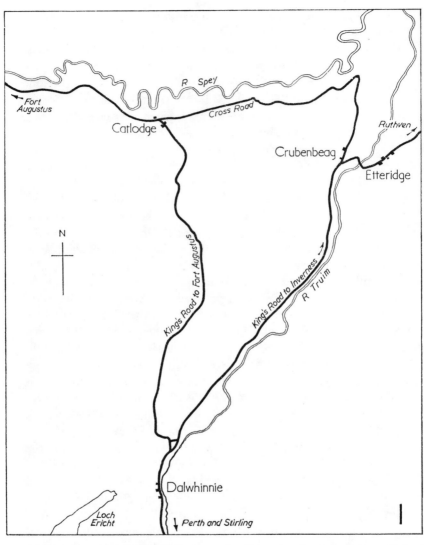

1 Dalwhinnie–Etteridge–Catlodge area (based on Roy's Survey). Roy had obviously no doubt at all about the line of the cross road between Ruthven and the Corrieyairack

not imply a road specifically built between these two places in a direct line, but rather communication between these areas along the roads already built.

After a very thorough examination of the ground and of the written and cartographic evidence available, the writer has no doubt at all that the line must have been along the existing road from Ruthven Barracks by Milehouse of Nuide and Phoines to Etteridge, across the little bridge near Crubenbeg school, and thence by what is now a forestry road to join the minor road from the A9 at 37/35/693953 to Catlodge at 37/35/666934. With finances as they were, it was improbable that General Wade would have made a road from Ruthven to the Corrieyairack within visual distance of the existing Dunkeld to Inverness road, involving a crossing of the Spey, and saving only a few hundred yards. For the same reason it is equally improbable that the present B970 was a Wade road. The existing road to Etteridge added little, if anything, to the journey to Fort Augustus, and there is no reason to assume that it was not used.

In the post-Wade period of road building, the Phoines–Nuide line was abandoned in favour of a crossing of the Spey at Ralia, and a realignment by way of Newtonmore and Kingussie. This is the period when the B970 and the A86 were undoubtedly conceived and developed. To attribute them to General Wade is to strain credulity to the point of untenability.

How many more roads General Wade would have liked to make is conjectural, but there is in existence a survey of the route through Glen Feshie to link Ruthven with Braemar. There is no evidence that he pressed the Treasury to provide for this road, and no estimate of cost appears to exist, though the first step of having a detailed survey made had been taken. Unfortunately plans were carried no further, and despite periodic outbursts in the press, the Glen Feshie road remains unbuilt.

CHAPTER 5

The Caulfeild Roads

The Argyllshire Roads

Dumbarton to Inveraray

Much work was done by statute labour on the Argyllshire roads, before, during and after the time of military building, particularly in the Inveraray and Loch Awe areas. On 10 June 1730 the Commissioners of Supply ordered the purchase of tools for road repairs, 'Eighteen setts of Quarry Tooles bought, each set consisting of a Gavelock, Mell, two mattocks or picks, two wedges, two iron shovels, and a Glasgow Sped'. These sets were distributed with instructions that the roads should be at least 'nine foot broad', that ditches be constructed to carry away the water, and that in boggy ground the road be floated on brushwood.[1]

The first military construction was in 1743, when plans were made for a road between Dumbarton and Inveraray, by Lochlomondside as far as Tarbet, thence by Arrochar, Glen Croe and Cairndow, the estimated cost for forty-four miles being £4,258 12s 0d. On 1 July General Cope received orders to start with a survey by 'Mr Cawfeild Inspector of Roads', and was given £1,000 on account.[2]

There was good cooperation between the army and the county. On 5 June 1745 the commissioners, noting that the bridge tò be built over the Leven at Bonhill would be useful to the county, provided horses and blankets for the troops.[3] According to Pococke in 1760, there was a stone 'three miles from Lus [with] this inscription, "Colonel Lascelles regiment, May 1745," that regiment being employed in this part of the road'.[4] Burt remarked that part of Campbell's regiment which was working on the road was taken by surprise by McGregor of Glengyle when the '45 started.[5] From this time until after Culloden no road work was undertaken but, as already noted, Albemarle was pressed into resuming work as soon as possible. Between October 1746 and February 1747 Caulfeild received £1,950 for the work done.[6] As he received a further £600 in May 1747, it seems that work was carried on during the winter, a point reinforced by General Churchill's letter to Newcastle that, in Caulfeild's opinion, if money was not immediately forthcoming, 'several bridges now building' might be destroyed by the delay, adding that there were '450 soldiers and artificers at work'.[7]

In June 1747 Caulfeild complained to Churchill about the transfer of one of his officers, Lieutenant Cunningham, who was 'well-acquainted with the Gentlemen of Dunbartonshire, and is very servicable in procuring Gravelling, Carts provisions and other things necessary'. Asking for his return Caulfeild continued, 'if officers are relieved as often as I have shown them what they are about, the work will be stop'd, and my toil more than I shall be able to undergo'. On 17 July the officer was posted back to him.[8]

During 1747 Caulfeild received £4,200 for work on this road, and in November was instructed by General Bland to carry on until Christmas. It was estimated in the same letter that a further £1,800 would be needed to finish the road. Work must have continued after Christmas because there were warrants for Caulfeild to draw gunpowder for blasting in February, and in April 1748 he got a further £500. In a letter some months later Caulfeild remarked that a party of '50 miners, wallers and quarriers worked by General Bland's Order all last winter on this side of Loch Fine under Ensign McCorkell'.[9]

Despite all this activity the road was not completed in 1748, but it had reached the top of Rest and Be Thankful in Glen Croe, where the original summit stone bore the date 1748.[10] In this year the tenants of Ardkinglas were ordered to attend with horses for four days 'for gravelling the road now carried on at the King's expense when they shall be required'.[11] This slow progress was one of the main criticisms levelled at Caulfeild by General Bland referred to in Chapter 2.

A War Office Order of 1749 detailed 150, later increased to 200, of Ancrum's regiment, stationed in Edinburgh, to finish the remaining twelve miles to Inveraray, and this they seem to have done, the tenants of Glenaray giving four days' service with horses carrying gravel.[12]

Towards the end of summer, Caulfeild, desperately short of money, wrote to Churchill's aide-de-camp that he would have to leave the bridge at Inveraray unfinished, hinting that 'this will hurt a great man for the bridge is at his door'. This hint was effective, because on 14 September he reported that the 'Inverara Bridge had been re-assumed . . . as a serviss to a great Man'.[13] Although money was made available for this purpose, he complained that 'all the Bridge builders and meal moneys are standing', and that he would have to leave 'with shame'. The sum involved was about £1,000. During 1749 nine bridges had been built between Ardkinglas and Inveraray by Thomas Clark, a Dunkeld mason, at a cost of £136, the 'Bridge of Ganan' costing a further £337 7s 4d.[14] In 1750 the tenants of Ardkinglas and Glenshirra had to do maintenance on the completed road.[15] In one way or another this road had caused Major Caulfeild more trouble than any other road before or after.

In 1763 a party of the 32nd Foot (the Duke of Cornwall's Light Infantry) repaired 2,157yd between Luss and Inveraray.[16] In 1768 the 93rd regiment recorded its work on the present stone at the top of Rest and Be Thankful. Both Pococke and Pennant were impressed by this road.[17] Between 1770 and 1784 annual military parties worked on the road at a total cost of over £4,200. Nearly £7,000 was spent on the Aray bridge, 'carried away' in 1773, and on the Leven bridge at Dumbarton.[18] In 1796 maintenance on roads in this area cost nearly £300 and the building of a three-arch bridge over the Froon near Dumbarton over £900. Between then and 1813 over 1,000yd of alterations were done on Lochlomondside because it had been impossible to make back drains, so that the road 'was the only conductor for rain water to the Loch', and the gravel was washed away. The Argyllshire part of this road was handed over to the Commissioners for Highland Roads and Bridges under the Road Repair Act of 1814, and in the following year 'breastwalls' were built along the edge of Loch Fyne and Loch Long.[19] Dunbartonshire did not take advantage of the 1814 Act, and in 1819 Southey complained that 'the jolting was such that with one accord we pronounced the Dunbartonshire roads to be worse than the Perthshire'.[20]

Tarbet to Crianlarich

It had been obvious to General Wade that cross roads linking the main arterial routes were essential, and this fact had not escaped Major Caulfeild. Roads had been or were being built between Dumbarton and Inveraray, and between Stirling and Fort William. The Inveraray road turned away from Lochlomondside at Tarbet to make for Arrochar. Sixteen miles to the north the Fort William road passed through Crianlarich at the end of the natural routeway through Glenfalloch from Loch Lomond. From the start this road was military. The Commissioners of Supply do not appear to have been interested until the establishment of a turnpike in 1829.[21] On 19 May 1752 General Churchill instructed Major Bernard of the Royal Welch Fusiliers in Glasgow to prepare a detachment of 350 for road work, and to send an advance party to Tyndrum to mark out the route under the direction of the engineer. It appeared, however, that 'Major Caulfeild intended to set the Welsh Fusiliers to work on Glenfalloch, etc.', which was confirmed by Churchill's aide on 24 May. On 9 June three barrels of gunpowder were sent to Inversnaid for use on the road. Unfortunately the Fusiliers had to go south on 1 September, so Caulfeild was given permission to make up the 'deficiency of the Fusiliers in their compliment of days' by using detachments of Skelton's and the King's regiments.[22]

In 1753 troops did not start work until 18–20 June. Bury's regiment was detailed to provide five companies and Bocland's regiment three 'to finish the Tarbet road' and work on 'the Brandry road'.[23] However, a further warrant issued for '65 Foot Tents with Poles, Pins, Mallets and Hatchets for the use of 5 Compan[ys] of Lt. Gen. Wolfe's Regiment who were to be employed in Finish[g] the road leading from Fort William to Tarbet, and the Brandery road'.[24] It is probable that the road was finished in this year apart from some bridges.

In 1757 Caulfeild received £5,209 1s 4d for 'carrying on the new roads in the Highlands', among which roads was that from Dumbarton to 'Glenfalloch and Inverara'.[25] The road was certainly completed by 1760 because Pococke, then in Tarbet, wrote that 'from Torbut the road goes off to Inveraray in the west, another military road going northward to Fort William 63 miles'.[26] In 1763 this road was repaired, including some realignment, by five NCOs and forty men of the 32nd Regiment of Foot. It was also one of those repaired regularly between 1770 and 1784.[27] In 1827 the Turnpike Trustees of Perthshire persuaded John Mitchell, Telford's Inspector of Roads, to supervise the conversion of the road into a turnpike. The work was carried out by D. McGregor of Tyndrum, employing 195 men at a cost of £3,480 in 1828. Toll bars were erected at the 'March Dyke between Crianlarich and Coiletter, and 100 yards north of Inverarnan', the Coiletter part being designated as a new line of road.[28]

Inveraray to Tyndrum

Caulfeild's road from Dumbarton had ended at Inveraray, but it was logical to carry it on to join the Stirling to Fort William road. The line from Inveraray was quite clear as far as Dalmally, but after that there was a choice between Glen Orchy, joining the Fort William road at Bridge of Orchy, or going by Glen Lochy to join up at Tyndrum. Either route was acceptable but, as in the case of the railway in later times, the Glen Lochy route was chosen. It is, of course, reasonable to assume that in summer, parties of soldiers going to Fort William would use Glen Orchy as a short cut. From Inveraray to Tyndrum by Glen Lochy was twenty-two miles. As early as 1747 Lord Glenorchy wrote to Campbell of Barcaldine, 'I think your project of the road thro' Glen Lochy is preferable to that thro' Glenorchy, and a road striking off to Bunaw would be very proper'.[29]

In his memorial of September 1749 Caulfeild had forecast that a road from Inveraray to Tyndrum 'passing thro' an Inhabited Country may be finished in One year by 400 men'.[30] But it took much longer. In 1750 and 1751, troops helped by the tenants of Glenorchy parish were working between Inveraray and Dalmally, while the tenants of Innishail, Kilchrennan, Ardchattan and Muckairn had to give three days' service on the road through Lettirbean. This was probably work done for the Commissioners of Supply who, as in other counties, paid military parties for road work. Certainly the commissioners between 1753 and 1755 paid Ensign Campbell the standard 2s 6d per day as overseer.[31] Full military construction was delayed until 1757, when Caulfeild got money 'for the new road from Inveraray to Tyndrum'.[32] Progress must have been slow because Pococke wrote in 1760, 'I set out from Inveraray and went by the Military road which is continued five miles to the west on the side of the hill over the Aray.'[33] No work seems to have been done at the Tyndrum end at this time. However, completion of the remaining seventeen miles was regarded as the main work for 1761. In Lord Ligonier's Order Book there is an entry over Caulfeild's signature for 'Four subaltern officers, eight serjeants, eight corporals, four drummers, and two hundred private men' to make 'the new road begun by order of his Royal Highness the Duke of Cumberland in 1757, and continued in 1760 by Field Marshall Lord Ligonier, between Inverara and Tynedrum'. In this year expenditure was just under £5,000. Soldiers were still on the same rate as in Wade's time, but smiths, carpenters and masons had received an increase of 6d per day. Even the hire of a horse and cart had risen from 4s 6d to 5s per day. This road was probably completed in 1761, because it was repaired in 1763 by a party from the 32nd Foot.[34] Thereafter it appears regularly in the lists of roads repaired.

There is a branch of this road from Dalmally through the Pass of Brander to Bonawe, not far from the blast furnace which had been set up, and which Pennant, in 1774, feared would 'soon devour the beautiful woods'.[35] The troops at work on this road in 1750 and 1751 were probably paid by the Commissioners of Supply.[36] In the following year a detachment of Bocland's regiment worked on it, and in 1754 Lieutenant General Wolfe's regiment was employed in finishing the road.[37] In 1768 it was damaged by the Argyll Furnace Company dragging timber along it, and it was one of the roads regularly repaired between 1770 and 1783.[38] The Bonawe road may well have been the one mentioned by Johnson when making his way from Mull to Inveraray: 'for half the day the ground was rough . . . In the latter part of the day we came to a firm and smooth road made by the soldiers, on which we travelled with great security.'[39]

Stirling to Dumbarton

The necessity for a line of communication between the key military posts of Stirling and Dumbarton is strategically obvious, and it would be fatuous to believe that there was no road between these two places before the eighteenth century. The original road went from Stirling by what is now a minor road, through Cambusbarron, joining the A811 at 54/51/742941 and forking left after about half a mile through Gargunnock and Kippen. It then followed the A811 through Buchlyvie and Drymen to Dumbarton.

From 1770 to 1784 there were military working parties on this road for the full ninety-two-day period every year at a total cost of £6,000.[40] While it is obvious that this was one of the roads on which the army and the counties must have worked together, there is no documentary proof. The only relevant reference in the minutes of the Commissioners of Supply for Stirlingshire is a promise, dated 30 April 1773, to compensate for damage to land caused by widening of the roads.[41] It is believed locally that the military work between 1770 and 1784 was mainly the realignment of the road along the A811, and although written evidence is lacking, the hypothesis is sound and completely credible. After 1790 the army disclaimed further responsibility and the road became a charge on the counties.

Stirling to Fort William

Direct access between Stirling and Fort William, an obvious requirement, was planned by way of Callendar, Lochearnhead, Crianlarich, Bridge of Orchy, the Devil's Staircase and Kinlochleven, a distance of ninety-three miles, much of it through difficult country. A start was made from both ends, and on 20 July 1748 a warrant was issued 'upon the Storekeeper of Stirling Castle to Maj^r Caulfeild or Mr Jas Campbell for such quantities of Powder as they may require for Carry^g on the Road to Down'.[42] That summer sixteen miles were built, three from Fort William and thirteen from Stirling.

A document of 1749 showed 300 men of Pulteney's regiment working from Lochearnhead towards the Pass of Leny and 300 of Sackville's working from the Pass of Leny towards them. They made about fifteen miles of road, but there is no record of troops working from the other end. At this stage the records become confusing. Caulfeild claimed in his report of 16 September 1749 that sixty miles of this road had been completed. On the other hand, a War Office document put the figure at forty-five miles.[43] The position was clarified by Caulfeild's report of 1750 which stated:

> The detachment from Colonel Rich's Reg[t] consisting of three Captains Seven Subalterns, ten Serj[ts], ten Corp[lls], three drums and 293 men work'd from the village of Mamore, near Fort William, towards Sterling and compleated four miles and a half. The detachment from Lt General Guise's Regim[t] consisting of one Captain Two Subalterns 3 Serj[ts] 3 Corp[lls] one drum and 112 Men work'd likewise from Mamore towards Sterling, and compleated two Miles and an half.[44]

Seven miles from Mamore towards Stirling meant the building of the notorious Devil's Staircase, and implies that the seven and a half miles from Blarmachfoldach to Mamore may have been made in the previous year. Meanwhile a detachment of Bocland's regiment comprising 9 officers and 365 other ranks 'work'd from the Head of Loch Earn over the Mountain of Largilie [Lairig Eala], towards Fort William, and compleated ten miles and fifty yards'.[45] This means that the road must have been made as far as Kingshouse in the west and Ben More in the east. A map drawn by the engineer, Harry Gordon, in 1751, shows that five companies of Rich's regiment and five companies of the Buffs continued the road under the shadow of Ben More, past Crianlarich and Tyndrum to Auch at the foot of Ben Dorain. They appear to have bridged the Orchy, and may have continued the road to Inveroran, leaving a gap between Auch and Bridge of Orchy.[46]

Between 17 and 19 May 1752 General Churchill ordered a concentration of troops in the Tyndrum and Black Mount area. A food contractor was informed that 'as two Engineers go from hence so as to be at each end of the Black Mount by the 25th or 26th Inst. with detachments of forty or fifty men each, in order to march out the road and Reconnoiter the Ground before the parties begin to work, it is General Churchill's order that you have meal in Readiness against their arrival'.[47] The officer commanding Bury's regiment was ordered to provide 200 men 'to March so as they may arrive at Maryburgh [Fort William] by the 27th Inst. . . . order a Subaltern and twenty men to meet Mr Baugh Engineer at the Head of Lochleven upon the 26th Inst. to assist him in marking out the Road, building Smith's forges, etc. A Commissary will be there to supply them with meal.'[48] Lochleven was merely a meeting-place, because they were ordered to 'encamp on such ground at Black Mount on 31st Inst as will be shown you by Mr Baugh Engineer'.[49] A similar order was sent to Colonel Crawfurd in Fort William to send a detachment of 10 officers and 370 other ranks to report to Mr Baugh.[50] From Perth a force of 3 officers and 110 other ranks, including an advance party, were to report to Mr Gordon, engineer, at Tyndrum, then encamp at Black Mount on 31 May.[51] A composite force of 10 officers and 370 other ranks, including two companies from Edinburgh, were to assemble at Stirling, send their advance party to Mr Gordon, and then encamp at Black Mount on 31 May.[52] The troops were encamped on each side of the Black Mount and worked towards each other. There were about 1,100 working on this part of the road in the summer of 1752, and on the road between Crianlarich and Tarbet there were 350 Welch Fusiliers. In his orders to Captain Murray for his two companies the general's aide showed a fine mixture of humanity and necessity; 'send as much Silver as possible, there being no such thing as Change to be got near the Black Mount'.[53]

By the middle of August, Harry Gordon, the engineer, reported that the road would be finished sooner than expected, which prompted General Churchill to suggest that two detachments could be used for repairs to the 'old roads'.[54] The general then informed the Secretary at War that as the road would be finished 'this week', the troops would work on the 'Tarbat road till their compliment of days are finished'.[55] At the same time his aide told Major Caulfeild how delighted the general was with the 'expedition with which the troops have worked'.[56] Unfortunately the weather then broke on the Black Mount and it was reported that 'the Detachments of Lt Gen Pulteney's and Lord Bury's have suffered greatly from the inclemency of the weather and that their tents are absolutely rotten'. It was left to the discretion of the officer commanding whether they went to work on the Tarbet road or went into winter quarters.[57] On 19 September the weather forced Bury's regiment to stop work a fortnight early. This caused some discontent among the troops at losing a fortnight's extra pay, believing that, having put up with conditions for so long, another two weeks would make little difference! It is, however, to Churchill's credit that he was genuinely concerned about their health.[58]

The road was not completed in 1752, and in the following April six companies of Bocland's regiment were detailed to finish it. Work did not start until 20 June, but there must have been very little to do, because they were able to send half of their number to the Glenfalloch road.[59] In 1754 General Bland, once more commander-in-chief, wrote to Caulfeild, 'I have sent an order to Ensign McCorkel to meet a Serjeant and 18 men of Wolfe's at Tyondrom road to take Charge of Repairing the Black Mount Road upon him, but by what I can hear of it is not a great repair wanted'.[60] On 21 May 1755 the storekeeper at Inverness was ordered to issue sixteen tents with camp equipment to a detachment of Beauclerk's regiment who were to repair the Black Mount road.[61] In 1763 a party of the 32nd Foot was working between Tyndrum and Bridge of Orchy clearing the scree washed down from Ben Dorain.[62] Between 1770 and 1784, working parties, at first of 100 and latterly of only 20, did annual repairs and maintenance at a total cost of £7,000.[63]

In 1774 Pennant had some interesting things to say about this road.

> [He] left Fort William and proceeded South along the military road on the side of a hill an awful height above Loch Leven . . . [the Lairig Mòr]. Immediately after leaving Kinlochleven the mountains soar to a far greater height than before: the sides covered with wood, and the bottoms of the glens filled with torrents that roar among the loose stones. After a ride of two miles begin to ascend the black mountain, in Argyleshire, on a steep road, which continues about three miles almost to the summit, and is certainly the highest publick road in Great Britain. On the other side the descent is scarce a mile, but is very rapid down a zig-zag way. Reach the King's House, seated in a plain: it was built for the accommodation of troops . . . the roads are excellent: but from Kinlochleven to Fort William very injudiciously planned . . . whereas had the engineer followed the track used by the inhabitants, these inconveniencies would have been avoided.[64]

Although mistaking the Devil's Staircase for the Black Mount, Pennant captured the atmosphere of this spectacular but difficult road. Only eleven years after he wrote, the Devil's Staircase and the Lairig Mòr were abandoned for a route through Glencoe, across the ferry at Ballachulish, and thence along the coast by Onich. This involved twenty-five miles of road and eight bridges, and cost £750.[65]

The minister of Glenorchy was critical of the military roads passing through his parish: 'the obvious and proper line was not always selected. The traveller often feels to his cost that the road was brought to the gravel and not the gravel to the road.'[66] It is easy to agree with the reverend gentleman writing in an age when roads were increasingly thought of as purely for the convenience of the civilian population, and in such a context he was right. But it must be remembered that these roads were conceived in a different atmosphere and built for a different purpose. Military and civilian requirements are not always coincident.

This road required constant attention, and the accounts of Sir Charles Preston in 1796 show that maintenance was costly. In that year no fewer than six road parties and three bridge parties were at work repairing and realigning. The cost for the season was over £1,500, giving a rate of almost £20 per mile, which gave some concern to their Lordships of the Treasury.[67] Between 1798 and 1813 six miles of alterations were made and seven bridges rebuilt in Glendochart. Two and a half miles of alteration took place near Tyndrum and two bridges were rebuilt. At Auch 1,000yd of realignment was needed as the road was not only being 'overwhelmed by scree pouring down from Ben Dorain', but was also being washed away by the river. There followed an enlightened and prophetic *cri du coeur* from the Road Commissioners that 'there is no way of preventing such frequent interruptions . . . but by altering the line of the road to the opposite side of the valley for about five miles'.[68] This dream was finally realised when the new road was made from Tyndrum to Ballachulish in the 1930s. At this time the commissioners favoured the proposal by Telford and the Highland Society to abandon the route through Glencoe and substitute for it a road from Glen Spean by Loch Trieg, Rannoch Moor and Glen Lyon, which would have been about fifteen miles shorter. But the landowners would not impose the necessary assessment and the project was never launched, though part of it later became the route of the West Highland Railway.[69]

The road from Tyndrum to Ballachulish, being in Argyllshire, was handed over to the commissioners under the terms of the Road Repair Act of 1814, but the part from Tyndrum to Callendar, being in Perthshire, was not handed over. Repairs to the Argyllshire sector in 1815 came to a modest £4 per mile.[70] In 1816 the commissioners had this to say about the road:

From the ferry at Ballachulish to the bottom of the valley, the Road has been cleared of large stones, the side drains have been cleared, and the Road by gravelling brought to regular shape; up the steep and rugged glen the Road has been rendered as perfect as it can be made without changing its direction. From the top of the Glen to the Kingshouse, the Road is brought into shape, and is smooth, but its direction is bad; nor could this be remedied, but by a new road for a space of two miles. From Kingshouse to Inveroran over the Black Mount, the Road . . . is now inferior to none in the North. From Inveroran to the head of Glenorchy, the Road is excellent; but at this place, commences a series of steep hills, which might be avoided . . . or improved . . . From Auch, ascending along a steep hill side, the Road passes over sundry steep ridges . . . From the summit to Tyndrum being in Perthshire, the Road . . . is in a bad state.[71]

The commissioners in 1821 alluded to a side effect of the Highland Clearances on road maintenance. Referring to the constant blocking of Glencoe by torrents washing down stones on to the road, they reported:

This sort of damage to the Road and to the Valley is said to have been unknown, until the Black Cattle, formerly depastured thereabouts, were supplanted by sheep, whose habit of ranging on higher ground, disturbs and sets in motion the rocky rubbish of the summit before it is decomposed by the weather; moreover, the passage of the water down the steep side of the mountain being interrupted by horizontal sheep tracks, it thereby acquires increased power of moving stones.[72]

It is a fitting footnote to an oft-maligned road that, after improvement between Kingshouse and Altnafeadh, a coach service plied at a profit after 1843 between Glasgow and Fort William over the Black Mount and through Glencoe.[73]

Coupar Angus to Fort George

On 16 August 1743 the Commissioners of Supply for Perthshire paid £15 to Farquarson of Rochalzie and Farquarson of Invercauld, who claimed to have made the road from Aberdeenshire to the Spittal of Glenshee 'commodious and fit for wheel carriages'. Some months later they paid £72 to Alexander Robertson of Straloch for repairing the Bridge of Cally some years before.[74] Despite this, Major Caulfeild decided that a military road was required to connect Perth and Dundee with the newly planned Fort George on Ardersier Point. This was no high-handed military action. In spite of repairs the Bridge of Cally was unsafe, and although Caulfeild had the advantage of being able to employ cheap labour, even he would have found that £15 would not have gone very far towards the cost of making a road fit for carriages. This is not to say that the Farquarsons were dishonest. It was purely a matter of standards. They firmly believed that their repairs had made the road suitable for wheeled vehicles, but what they considered adequate fell below the acceptable military standard, an interesting point for those who derogate the military roads. This road, when the addition from Blairgowrie to Coupar Angus is included, was almost 100 miles long. Caulfeild had no doubt that the road should run from Blairgowrie, by the Spittal of Glenshee, to Braemar. From there, however, to Fort George, the ideal line had to be weighed against cost before a final solution was reached. Communication from Blairgowrie to the south was regarded as adequate, though at a later date the road was extended back to Coupar Angus.

On 20 July 1748 a warrant was issued 'upon the Officer Command[g] the Train at Perth' to supply Major Caulfeild with such powder as he required for making the road from Blairgowrie to Braemar, but there is no record of anything being done during that year. At the same time the new Fort George was planned 'at Adeseapoint in Scotland [Ardersier], with an estimate of the charge'. Building was started the following year, Barrel's regiment providing the military labour.[75]

In 1749, 300 men of Guise's regiment were set to work between Braemar and the Spittal of Glenshee, while a party of the Welch Fusiliers worked north from Blairgowrie to meet them. This party reached Dalrulzion, while the northern party got down four miles south of the Spittal. In his report of September 1749 Caulfeild stated that twenty-four miles were made, leaving a gap of about six miles between the parties. He also gave a list of the nineteen bridges built at a cost of £549, including two with arches of fifty-two feet, one to replace the old Bridge of Cally, and the other at the Spittal of Glenshee. A bridge with a thirty-foot arch was put across the Cluny. These bridges were built by James Robertson, a mason from Dunkeld.[76]

In 1750 Caulfeild reported:

The detachment from Lord Bury's regiment . . . work'd between Blairgowrie and Castleton of Braemar and compleated near six miles joining the roads begun last year . . . they likewise repair'd a good deal of the road made last season and made 520 yards side Pavement. No party have worked better since I have been employed. Capt Trapeau commanding Officer, Mr Morrison Engineer.

He then went on to discuss the road beyond Braemar:

The distance between the Castle of Braemar and the Castle of Cargarff measures Sixteen miles as by the Survey Number 1. The first Six Miles on the Side of the River Dee has been already in some measure made by the shire of Aberdeen and may be easily made a very good road.

Thereafter he favoured a route suggested by Colonel Watson,

which runs some Miles farther along Deeside to Cromar, where it turns up an inhabited glen to Cargarff. This is some miles about but the Colonel says it is very practicable.[77]

But it must have been decided that such a diversion was too great and too expensive, because the road was given a more direct line, by Gairnshiel, where a bridge was necessary, then by Allt Glas–Choille and Delachuper to Corgarff.

An interesting footnote to the Braemar road appears in General Bland's Letter Book for 1756. Half a mile of road had not been made, 'occasioned by a Field through which it was to pass having been covered with Corn the time the rest of the road was made'. The Commander of Braemar garrison was ordered to finish it. Caulfeild would supply the tools and pay the men 'in the usual manner'.[78] Evidently troops employed even casually on road work were entitled to additional pay.

As Major Caulfeild had indicated in his survey of 1750, there was little choice of route between Corgarff and Grantown on Spey. The distance was twenty-three miles, 'mostly through Muirs and spungy ground and will require many ditches and side drains, and will take full 800 men to make this road in one season'. From Grantown Caulfeild favoured keeping to the east of the Findhorn and crossing by ferry at Forres. As the ground was dry and 'gravelly . . . 500 men may easily compleat . . . in Ninety Two Days'. He roundly condemned the practice of dragging timber along the roads, citing Sir Ludovic Grant as a particular sinner, as it made channels in the gravel for rain water 'which then gathers into Currants and destroy all before them'.

A survey numbered 'Three' showed that the Findhorn could be safely bridged at a number of points. A bridge at Dulsie would make the road eight miles shorter than if the bridge were at Culterness, and a bridge at Culterness would need an eighty-foot arch and would cost £600. Dulsie Bridge would cost £150, but a bridge at Rheny would cost £300. The Culmoney Bridge would cost £250 but, as at Dulsie, the approaches would be difficult. Caulfeild repeated that he preferred a road east of the Findhorn, which would also be cheaper, but added, 'the Gentlemen who live on each side of the Findhorn give their opinion for the situation of the bridge and line of the road as their several Reasons induce them. My view is to lay the whole truely before H.R.H. and to do my duty to the best of my Judgement.'[79] Influential local opinion (not for the first or last time) must have prevailed. The Dulsie line (the cheapest bridge!) was chosen, thence the road went in a fairly straight line by Cawdor to Fort George.

Argument as to the best line led to a hold-up, but work was resumed in 1753, when construction of the Braemar to Corgarff section was undertaken by four companies of Holmes's regiment, while two companies of Beauclerk's and one company of Skelton's worked north of Corgarff.[80] This was also the year of building the big five-arch bridge at Invercauld, the *Aberdeen Journal* of 24 July reporting injuries to workmen and a fatal accident during the course of blasting operations. From the same source it appears that the Lecht road was started that year.

The year 1754 was one of activity. In March five companies of Lord Charles Hay's regiment and five companies of Holmes's drew tents and camping equipment. Leighton's regiment drew tents for two companies.[81] That meant over 700 men working on the road that summer. The stone at the Well of the Lecht indicates that this part of the road was built by 'Five companies of the 33rd Regiment, Honourable Lord Charles Hay, Colonel'. By the end of 1754 the road, including the bridge over the Spey at Grantown, was complete to that point.

General Bland's secretary wrote to Caulfeild in June of that year that Lieutenant Farquhar, commanding the detachment at Tomintoul, reported that the hut used by officers was the property of Gordon of Glenbucket who, with a certain amount of malice, had put in a tenant, 'which greatly dustressed Mr Farquhar, having no other place to live in'. Caulfeild was ordered to send a party of Lord Charles Hay's regiment to build a 'convenient Hutt to serve Mr Farquhar and his successors for 5 or 6 years without incurring any unnecessary expence'. A month later the general, writing to compliment Caulfeild for his initiative in regravelling the road made the previous year, advised him that the Duchess of Gordon would give him ground at Tomintoul for a hut.[82]

Work continued on the final twenty-eight miles in 1755 and, apart from building Dulsie Bridge, this must have been the easiest part of the road. In May an order was issued for forty-six tents 'for the use of three Companies of Ld Robt Manner's Regt to be employed in finishing the new Road from Brae-mar to Fort George'.[83] As parts of the road near Nairn may well have been existing civilian roads requiring only repair work, the main job of construction may possibly have been completed in that year. There is no mention of work being done in 1756, but General Anstruther's regiment drew sixty tents for 'carrying on the works at Fort George'.[84] It is certain that the road was finished by 1757, because in that year, apart from the completion of some bridges, the main work was the painting and figuring of the mile-stones.

At the end of the road was the new Fort George. Work progressed and in 1753 there were fifteen companies at work. Pococke in 1760 reported, 'it is the design of Colonel Skinner . . . Three sides of a Court for Barracks are finished . . . near the entrance are to be the houses of the Governor and Deputy Governor; there are sluices to let in sea water on the South Side, and make it an island'.[85] Fort George was something of a white elephant because it never saw a shot fired in anger, but it remains a wonderful and indestructible monument to the eighteenth-century art of military fortification. The senses reel in imagining the cost of such a complex in the twentieth century.

At the Blairgowrie end of the road the need was then felt for better communication with Coupar Angus and the south. A handsome bridge was built over the Isla, but in 1766 Caulfeild wrote to the Perthshire commissioners that 'the Bridge built over the Isla last year will be inaccessible to wheel'd Carriages till a road is made to each end of it'. He offered every possible assistance and the fullest cooperation with local labour. In truth the road from the 'Water of Illa to Blairgowrie' had been repaired by the county in 1758, which again emphasises the point that what had satisfied the county was sub-standard to Major Caulfeild.[86]

This part of the road and the bridge are mentioned in the account of the parish of Bendochy in the *Old Statistical Account*:

> There was a bridge built over the Isla . . . by the Government . . . The arches are 5. The middle arch is 30 feet above the summer water; and the road is over 15 feet wide . . . The bridge is built over the only two natural great stones in the river, called the riding stone and the wading stone; and as works of nature outlive those of art, they may shew the place where it stood after it is gone.[87]

Fortunately, that day has not yet come. Between 1770 and 1784 military parties did the annual repair work, the overall expenditure being £6,900, including major repairs to the Isla and Grantown bridges.[88] Sir Charles Preston's accounts show that repairs in 1796 came to over £425. During the period from 1798 to 1813 alterations were made in the Blairgowrie and Braemar areas. The Blairgowrie works were of a major nature involving the six miles between Lornty Bridge and Bridge of Cally,

> to avoid a steep, narrow, dangerous tract of road . . . the Cloves of Mawes, winding like a corkscrew from Blairgowrie to the summit of a steep hill [a distance of nearly two miles] and descending with fearful steepness to the Bridge of Cally. This road was worse than . . . the Devil's Staircase.

This was a gross exaggeration, but the minister of Blairgowrie was also a critic of this part of the road in the *Old Statistical Account*.[89] After the Road Repair Act of 1814 this road disappears from the list of those maintained by the Commissioners for Highland Roads and Bridges, except for the Morayshire section.

Coupar Angus to Dunkeld and Amulree

The east to west cross roads were important links in the chain of military roads. In this category are the two short roads which together form a link between the Coupar to Fort George road, the Dunkeld to Inverness road and the Stirling to Dalnacardoch road. A road existed between Coupar and Dunkeld and between Dunkeld and Amulree long before the military authorities had any ideas on the subject. Both roads are listed as military, but the actual military construction seems to be minimal. Roy shows no road by Caputh from Coupar to Dunkeld, but shows a definite line through Strath Bran from Dunkeld to Amulree. Both roads are shown by Taylor and Skinner.

There is no record showing work being done by military units between Coupar and Dunkeld, but the road always appears on lists in the latter part of the eighteenth century as a military road. It first appears in the Minutes of the Commissioners of Supply for Perthshire in 1753, when a petition for repairs was considered. In this and in subsequent entries it is referred to as a road, not as a *new* road, when the commissioners require the parishes of Caputh, Cluny and Lethendy to carry out repairs, as a regular duty.[90] In 1765 an intriguing entry refers to a road north from Essendy by Kirk of Kinloch to Bridge of Cally 'to join the military road'.[91] Does this mean that even though the Coupar to Dunkeld road was listed as military, the commissioners did not regard it as such, because they were responsible for its maintenance? There is no record of military parties doing repairs or of a grant to the commissioners for upkeep.

The continuation of this road through Dunkeld to Amulree appears in Lord Ligonier's Order Book as one of the roads 'carried on' in 1761. Obviously a military party had been working on it that year, but the county had been dealing with the road since 1735, and the bridges seemed to have caused a lot of trouble. In 1740 the bridge over the Bran was swept away by the spate before it was completed and had to be rebuilt by three Dunkeld masons. In 1743 the 'Trustees appoint the Undertakers of the Bridge of Ballinloan to be prosecute before the private dustrict', because one side of the arch had fallen in 1737 and the other in 1743. It had been built by James Pirnie, mason, in 1735, at a cost of £163 16s, but he had died in 1737, so there were difficulties. At the same time the commissioners ordered repairs on the Strath Bran road, which had become almost impassable. They also 'allowed £441 Scots to complete the Bridge of Bran', making a total of £1,701 Scots (approximately £140 sterling). Whether or not the bridge fell down again is not clear, but in 1747 a letter was 'produced from Major Cawfeild' asking the commissioners to survey lines for building a bridge over the Bran. The commissioners agreed that the county should provide the necessary 'Carriage and Services'. It must have been obvious to the commissioners that it was better to provide transport for Caulfeild, who would ensure that the bridge would be properly built, rather than rely on the demonstrably shoddy workmanship from which they had been suffering. The point was reiterated in 1749 with a recommendation to all districts to give full support to Caulfeild in all road matters.[92]

The troubles which beset this little road were by no means over. For some reason the tenants of Ballinloan in 1751 'stoped up the Highway leading betwixt Ballinloan and Crief . . . by building fold dykes and throwing up a ditch'. This may have been because by this time the bridge was a total wreck, though the commissioners were considering estimates for rebuilding and were still contemplating action against the original builders of the bridge over the Bran. Regular repairs were carried out on the road by the commissioners, and in 1758 they again made the distinction of ordering repairs to the 'Strath Bran Road as far as till it meets the *King's* Road near Amulree'. It is significant that they ordered repairs in 1761 on what was listed as the *new* road from Inver to Amulree. This was the year when the road appeared in Ligonier's Order Book, and the entry could imply fairly extensive work by the soldiers. In the same year, in the House of Commons Journal, was recorded a payment of £57 7s for the 'repair of Bridges in Strath brand between Dunkeld and Amulree'. It is possible that the army was now paying for the bridges, while the county was responsible for the road.[93]

In 1756 there was a not irrelevant correspondence between General Bland and the Duke of Atholl. The Duke had proposed a road between Dowally Kirk and the Spittal of Glenshee, promising that he and other landowners would 'contribute the assistance of the Country People provided a Serjeant and 12 men are sent to instruct them in the method'. Bland promised to comply as soon as he heard what assistance to expect and what accommodation would be provided. The Duke must, however, have changed his mind, and his further proposal received the following reply from Bland:

As the Serj[t] and twelve men were ordered by H.R.H. the Duke to assist the Country People in the repair of the Road from the Kirk of Dowlie to the Spittle of Glenshee, I cannot take it on me to Direct them to work upon the road from Inver to Amallrie, but as the opening of the last Communication is certainly of Publick Utility, I should think the Duke of Atholl may; and all I can do in it is to order the Party to march from Perth to receive your Commands at Dunkeld, so soon as Tools can be sent from Leith for them.

At this point the correspondence seems to end, but as the Dowally road was not built, the military party must have been employed on the Inver to Amulree road, and so posterity was deprived of what would have been an interesting military road. On 3 May of the following year, the commissioners offered to make the Dowally road 'in conjunction with military parties', in place of the existing Moulin to Kirkmichael road, but the offer was not taken up.[94]

Between 1774 and 1778 sums amounting to over £300 were spent on repairing bridges between Dunkeld and Amulree from Treasury sources.[95] In 1774 the commissioners granted £10 sterling for the building of what came to be known as 'Rumbling Bridge' over the Bran, listed by Taylor and Skinner as 'New Bridge', an exercise which would have been pointless unless there was an intention to re-route the road on the right bank of the Bran by Trochrie (the present line), instead of continuing on the left bank by Ballinloan.[96] The road continued to be repaired jointly by the Commissioners of Supply and the army, as is evident from the 1796 accounts of Sir Charles Preston, but it was finally handed over to the county some time between 1798 and 1805.[97]

Fort Augustus to Bernera

The barracks at Bernera, probably completed in 1720, were among those established as a result of the 1715 Rising. They were built without the permission of the landowner, MacLeod of MacLeod, and the 'nastiness which was thrown out of the barracks' spoiled a salmon fishery producing ten to twelve barrels a year. MacLeod eventually, in 1749, received compensation of £1,600. According to Pennant, the brochs at Glenelg were pillaged to build the barracks. He found the buildings 'handsome and capacious, designed to hold two hundred men', but at the time of his visit in 1772, occupied only by a corporal and six soldiers. Boswell in 1773 and Knox in 1786 reported even smaller 'garrisons'.[98] After the barracks were given up by the army, a number of families, victims of the Clearances and in receipt of Kirk

Session poor relief, lived there, and in 1846 Glenelg Free Church was reputed to have been roofed with slates from the barracks.[99]

The position, controlling the narrows at Glenelg and the shortest crossing to Skye, was ideal, but it was forty-three miles to the nearest military road at Fort Augustus. Not only was communication with Fort Augustus necessary, but a 'road to the isles' would be a logical continuation of the Corrieyairack road from Dalwhinnie, through the central Highlands to the west coast. If only the Glen Feshie road had been made, there would have been a line of military road from east to west across the country.

A road from Fort Augustus to Bernera seems to have been planned as early as 1746, because there is a map of the route to be taken drawn by Daniel Paterson in that year. In his memorial of 1749 Caulfeild felt that this road 'may be made in *one* summer by 600 men'.[100] The estimate was, perhaps, over-sanguine, because the road took longer both to be started and to be finished, though, in fairness to Caulfeild, if 600 soldiers had been employed, his forecast might have been correct.

There is no record of any work being done until 1755, when a warrant was issued in May for Home's regiment to draw sixty-five tents, 'to be employed in making a road from Fort Augustus to Bernera'. In July the regiment had a warrant to draw two barrels of gunpowder for work on the road. According to the scale of tentage this was an operation involving five companies, about 300 men, only half the number Caulfeild had wanted. In the following year Leighton's regiment drew twelve tents for the detachment working on this road, enough for only one company. In a letter of 29 June 1756 General Bland ordered General Holmes to send a company at once to Fort Augustus from Inverness, because Governor Trapaud had informed him that after the Bernera road detachment left, he would not have sufficient troops to garrison the fort. The married men working on the Bernera road received two pecks of meal per week until the end of July, after which it was reduced to one and a half pecks, when 'provisions were more plentiful in the Country'. On 9 August, General Bland, giving instructions to Captain Rickson, who was to work with Caulfeild and later make the Galloway road, asked him to report on the progress made on the Bernera road.[101] This implies that the road was not completed in 1756.

The next positive mention of the Bernera road was in 1763, when a detachment of eighty men, commanded by a captain from the 21st Foot (the Royal Scots Fusiliers), made 5,289yd of road. They also made 5,488yd of back drain and 5,449yd of side drain.[102] It is not clear whether the extra yardage of back and side drains was a completion of work of the previous year, or preparation for the following year. Eighty seems a small number to be employed on actual road building. The figure resembles more that of a maintenance party; but there was a captain in command, with a subaltern to help. The amount of work done was recorded in yards, not miles, and this was how maintenance work was usually shown. The one clear point is that in 1763 work was being done on the Bernera road, and it was listed as 'making a new road'.

There is a dearth of information on this road until the 1770s. In 1770 ninety-two days' work by 2 subalterns and 100 men cost £292 17s 4d, but there is no indication whether the work was building or repairing. The detail was repeated in 1771. The following year the numbers were halved, but there was a supplementary sum of £470 to 'repair and re-build bridges carried away by extra-ordinary floods of November last . . . six were carried away and 12 are in danger of falling'. In 1774 there were additional charges of almost £500 for, *inter alia*, 'underground drains', implying significantly that the old open cross drain had been abandoned in favour of the culvert. Between 1770 and 1784 the expenditure on building and maintenance on the Bernera road was £6,100.[103]

Dr Johnson, in his journey to the western isles in 1773, used this road. Leaving Fort Augustus he wrote: 'we soon came to a high hill, which we mounted by a military road, cut in traverses . . . we found a party of soldiers from the fort, working on the road, under the superintendence of a serjeant'. He spent the night at the inn at Aonach, noticing that the soldiers he had met came to drink at it, 'having marched at least six miles to find the first place liquor could be bought'. The army estimates for 1770 included £80 for the building of this inn, as there was 'no house in fifty miles of the said line'. In the following year there was a further £60 for offices. The final cost of inn and stables was £159. Johnson described it as 'one of three huts . . . distinguished by a chimney . . . we . . . were conducted through the first room that had the chimney, into another lighted by a small glass window . . . Near it was a garden of turnips and a field of potatoes . . . his wealth consists of 100 sheep as many goats, and 28 beeves ready for the drovers'.[104] It is interesting to find potatoes as a field crop in such a remote part at this time.

The following day the travellers 'came to Ratikin [Ratagan] a high hill on which a road is cut, but so steep and narrow, that it is very difficult'. Boswell, in his *Journal of a Tour to the Hebrides*, found that Ratagan was 'terrible steep to climb, notwithstanding the road is formed slanting along it'. The only other inn on the road was over Ratagan at Glenelg, where there was 'no meat, no milk, no bread, no eggs, no wine . . . whisky we might have, and . . . at last they caught a fowl and killed it'. That night the good doctor had to sleep in his riding coat on a pile of hay. Boswell, 'being more delicate, laid himself sheets with hay over and under him, and lay in linen like a gentleman'.[105]

After 1784 there is no mention of military repairs to the road, and the barracks, which had long been occupied by a token force under a corporal, was abandoned in 1790. As soon as a road ceases to be maintained, deterioration is rapid. The minister of Glenshiel recorded in the 1790s that the 'military road from Fort Augustus to Bernera . . . has been neglected since 1776 [*sic*]. Before that period it was kept in repair by a party of soldiers.' The minister of Glenmoriston made a similar report, but the most interesting comment came from the minister of Glenelg:

> The roads are bad . . . The bridges were first erected by contractors, who made choice of those parts over the waters where materials could be had at cheapest rates; by this means the roads were unavoidably lengthened, and carried over steep and high precipices . . . This made the charge more troublesome to the military who laboured at the roads, that in no place or part was the road made sufficient or of proper dimensions . . . This line of road is the shortest from the metropolis to the island of Sky and the Long Island . . . From its present situation it is impossible to ride it, by this means travellers are necessitated to freight vessels from Argyleshire at an enormous expence.[106]

Bridge building by contract had also been done on the Inveraray to Tyndrum road without incurring the same criticism. Here the point is made that the contractors put the bridges, not in the best places, but where they would be cheapest to build, thereby leaving the soldiers with the unenviable task of connecting unsuitably sited bridges with lengths of road. It is difficult to believe that Caulfeild and his successors would have given contractors such a free hand, but the inspector could not be present all the time. Allowing for some exaggeration in the minister's statement, it is probable that there was some sharp practice by the profit-seeking contractors.

When Telford was doing his survey in 1802, he noted, 'I travelled along the *Vestiges* of a Military Road, up Glenshiel, down a part of Morrison, and over a rugged mountain to Fort Augustus.' In a later report he decided to use 'the deserted Military Road from Fort Augustus to Bernera Barracks, preserving nearly the same line from Bridge of Doe to Glenelg, which will serve to connect, though imperfectly, the disjoined parts which may first be executed'.[107] The new road came through Glen Moriston instead of over the top from Fort Augustus. From Achlain onwards it followed the line of military road but usually at a lower level. It was not finished until 1819, and the Kintail stretch of ten miles cost £1,000 per mile—a far cry from the days of Wade and Caulfeild. In view of all the authenticated work done on this road, it is puzzling to find the Commissioners of Supply for Inverness endorsing a statement made by the Highland Society in 1799 that 'this line of road is not yet made, though of very great public importance'.[108]

Contin to Poolewe

The fifty-two miles of 'military road' between Contin and Poolewe present a problem. Was there a road all the way? Was there a road part of the way? Was there a road at all? In fact, there is evidence of one kind or another to support all three contentions!

A good road from Inverness to Poolewe, whence there was access to Stornoway, would have been useful, and there is certainly evidence of military working parties in the area, the first being in Lord Ligonier's Order Book of 1761.[109] Two years later Lord George Beauclerk recorded that just over 5,000yd of 'new road from Canton to Pollow in Roshire' were made by ten NCOs and sixty men of the 8th Foot.[110] In 1767 Sir Alexander Mackenzie of Gareloch was empowered to call out all the inhabitants of the parish to repair the road, 'and where Soldiers are employed on any of the said roads that the Country people be obliged to provide them in bedding and Utensils for Dressing their Victuals'. Obviously the commissioners had no definite information whether there was to be a military presence or not. From 1770 until 1780 a military party worked each summer for ninety-two days at an overall cost of about £800, but there was no reference to bridges. Despite this the commissioners gave in 1777 'Ten pounds Sterling for purchasing Tools and paying an Overseer for the Road from Contin to Pollew'. 'As the said road is in great Disrepair', a further £7 10s 0d was made available.[111] From this there is no doubt that the army did some form of maintenance or construction between 1760 and 1780, but it is clear that fifty-two miles of road could not have been made according to existing standards by the number of men employed. There are definite traces of a road between Contin and Kinlochewe, with a fine military type of bridge at Garve, and there is a short stretch between Poolewe and the end of Loch Maree, possibly for the benefit of the iron works at Furnace.

Roy, in his survey, sketches a route from Contin to Poolewe along the north shore of Loch Maree, but Taylor and Skinner, in 1776, show nothing at all of any such road. The late Sir Alexander Mackenzie, in his article on the military roads, written for the Inverness Field Club, made the point that the road was regularly maintained by statute labour, but that there was no reference to military parties. He also recounted that in the latter part of the eighteenth century Lady Seaforth took her coach over this road, but had to abandon it wrecked on the south shore of Loch Achanalt.[112] In 1786 Knox commented: 'From [Inverness] northward . . . No soldier ever appeared for the purpose of making roads, excepting a small party, some years ago, near Loch Maree, which road they did not complete.'[113] The minister of Gairloch commented in 1792 that 'there are many rivers in this parish, but no bridges nor passage but by horses'. At the same time the minister of Contin made no mention of roads, but only of two ferrymen, one at Contin and another at the river Connon.[114]

In 1802 the Highland Society suggested to Telford the necessity of a road from Contin 'which already had a good road to Dingwall', routed along the south side of Loch Garve and the head of Loch Luichart to Acnasheen, with branches to Carron and Poolewe. In the map appended to the 6th Report of the Commissioners for Highland Roads and Bridges, dated 1813, there is no road shown between Contin and Poolewe.[115] The Loch Carron road was made, and in 1819 Southey noted, 'it is desirable that a road should be made there branching off from the Jeantown road at this place [Achanalt]'.[116] As late as 1828 the commissioners were debating 'the necessity of a road from Achnasheen to Poolewe, by the north side of Loch Maree', a distance of twenty-six miles at an estimated cost of £12,000. At the same time Mr Stewart Mackenzie of Seaforth offered to build such a road, 'where there is no road, but about a mile from Poolhouse, made within these last three years by me'.[117] In 1845 the minister of Gairloch, without giving details, complained of 'the want of roads'. In this year the Contin minister mentioned the 'parliamentary road' to Loch Carron, but said nothing of a road to Poolewe from Achnasheen.[118]

The evidence points to the possibility of some form of road between Contin and the eastern end of Loch Maree, but it is impossible to say when it was constructed or by whom. There is no evidence to suggest that it went all the way to Poolewe. The balance of contemporary opinion is to the contrary. Perhaps the only simple and certain fact about this road is that, if it was ever made, it was not built by General Wade!

The Northern Link Roads

In the area bounded by Inverness, Aviemore, Fort George and Grantown on Spey there is a network of short roads linking the major roads. There is little evidence of their construction by military hands, but they appear on lists of military roads and were repaired as such, and some of them were handed over to the Commissioners for Highland Roads and Bridges as military roads. In most cases they seem to have existed in at least a rudimentary form before being made up by the army as useful link roads.

Sluggan Bridge to Dulnain Bridge

When this road was made must be purely conjectural. Extensive alterations were made in 1802 between Duthil Kirk and Dulnain Bridge to make it the main road between Aviemore and Grantown.[119]

It provided a useful link between the original Wade road to Inverness and the Coupar Angus to Fort George road. The part from Sluggan Bridge to Carr Bridge was abandoned in favour of the new line from Aviemore to Slochd at the beginning of the nineteenth century.

Grantown to Aviemore

There are no details of military construction, but between 1780 and 1784 the government paid over £300 for the repair of bridges.[120] Writing in 1782, the minister of Duthil declared that the road from

Grantown to Aviemore, 13 miles in length, was repaired in 1779 to 24 feet in breadth, being formerly 12 feet, by the country people, at the request of the proprietor, Sir James Grant. The bridges were originally built at the expense of the proprietor; one of which, a stone bridge over the water of Dulnan of one arch, built in 1700, having now fallen into disrepair, is completely supplied by a bridge built last summer, 1791, close by it.[121]

If this report is accurate, the road had been maintained by local labour for at least twenty years. There is no suggestion that the 1791 bridge was military, yet in 1795 this road was being repaired as a military road. It was described by the commissioners as 'an imperfect military road' which they were prepared to repair 'at a considerable expence, considering that the extent of it does not exceed seven miles'. This refers to the part between Carr Bridge and Dulnain Bridge, which was being repaired as part of the 1796 programme. The Morayshire part of the road was handed to the commissioners under the 1814 Road Repair Act. After the alterations made between Carr Bridge and Dulnain Bridge, the original road between Aviemore and Dulnain Bridge was abandoned.[122]

Dulsie Bridge to Aviemore

From Dulsie Bridge through Dava Moor and past Lochindorb to Duthil, where it joined the Carr Bridge to Dulnain road, was a route which had been in existence long before military days, and it was an obvious short cut from Aviemore to Fort George. When and to what extent the army was concerned with the road is not clear, but there is a survey done by Cadet Gunner George Campbell, who was on duty in the area in the 1750s, sketching a road all the way to Boat of Garten from Fort George.[123] This may merely have been a plan of an existing road without implying military construction. In the early 1790s, according to the Duthil minister, the road was realigned, making it four miles shorter.[124] This was confirmed in a memorial from Major James Cunningham to the Commissioners for Highland Roads and Bridges in 1811, in which he made the point that 'Lord Eglinton, when Surveyor General of Roads [1788–94], made a great improvement by opening the present line from Aviemore to the Grantown road near Dulsie'.[125] It was repaired as a military road thereafter, and handed over by Morayshire to the commissioners in 1814.

Grantown to Forres

This road strikes off from the Coupar to Fort George road at Dava Bridge, crosses the Divie near its junction with the Findhorn, then follows the latter river to Forres. It had been considered by Caulfeild as one of the possible routes to Fort George. It was made and maintained by various hands. 'In 1783,' wrote the minister of Edenkillie, 'a sixty two foot arch bridge was built over the Divie for £220, £100 of which came from the Commissioners for Forfeited Estates'.[126]

Fort George to Inverness

There was little doubt that this road was built before the fort was completed, but there are no details of its construction by military hands. Afterwards it was always listed as a military road. The minister of Petty described it in 1792 as a military road 'made about 12 years ago by statute labour, but has lately been repaired and in some places altered in direction and 4 bridges built on it at public expense'.[127] There is no doubt at all that the road was in existence long before 1780. The minister may have been confused between actual building and handing over to the local authority.

The northern link roads are all logical lines of communication, and there is not the slightest doubt that the army used them, and shared in their upkeep. They were used by soldiers, who also worked on them from time to time and, above all, they were accepted by the government as military roads.

The Military Roads in the North-East

In the counties of Aberdeenshire, Banffshire and Kincardineshire there is a network of roads which may be described as military, in the sense that, after the '45, soldiers played some part in construction, maintenance, or both, for a number of years. It would be fatuous to suggest that populous counties such as these had no roads until the period of military occupation after the '45, but there is clear evidence of frequent military working parties in the middle of the eighteenth century.

In 1721 Banffshire appointed a General Surveyor of roads at a salary of £100, and in the following year levied a tax of ten shillings per £100 valued rent to supplement statute labour. This tax was levied every year until 1804, apart from the years of hardship after the '45, between 1747 and 1750, and some of it was used to build bridges on the route subsequently followed by the military road from Coupar to Fort George. In the confusion and hardship following the '45, county road work lapsed, but in 1751 the tax was reimposed and supplemented by Rogue Money. The equipment provided was scarcely on a lavish scale, 'three small coup carts, half a dozen wheelbarrows, two dozen spades and shovels, three small gavelocks, two mashes one bigg and another small, and half a dozen picks and one large sway'. Apart from gunpowder, the tools were the same as those described by Edmund Burt for military use. The commissioners advised all heritors 'that the roads be carried as streight as possible . . . not under fourteen feet of breadth besides a ditch on each side for carrying off the water'. The most significant part of the minute, however, was that after payment for the tools, the money should be used for 'payment of the soldiers or artificers to be employed for making out these roads'. In the following year the commissioners decided to apply for a sergeant and twelve men to work on the road from Banff to Boindie, 'on the expence of the county', with help from 'the inhabitants of Banff'. They also applied to General Churchill for 'four of the military or more if necessary' to help local labour on the Banff to Rothiemay road, to be paid from Rogue Money. Soldiers appear to have been employed until 1757. In that year the commissioners discovered that they had been overpaying the sergeant. 'There is eighteen pence per diem charged as given to the

Serjeant, the meeting are of opinion that it was too much, and therefore they resolve that hereafter they will not allow above a shilling to any serjeant to be employed.'[128]

As early as 1752 military parties were working in Aberdeenshire. On 19 September Churchill's aide ordered the officers commanding the garrisons at Braemar and Corgarff to send men to help the masons who were employed for the government in building a bridge over the Don, because 'the Country People being employed at their harvest . . . The men will be paid by the masons weekly for their work.' In October of the same year Churchill thanked a group of Aberdeenshire landowners, who had praised the efficiency of their military party, and assured them of his continuing goodwill, allowing them to retain a small quantity of powder left over. In 1753 a corporal and six to eight men were sent at the request of Sir Archibald Grant of Monymusk to repair the road there, with the proviso that 'Sir Archibald will pay them in the usual manner'. In the previous year the gentlemen of the lower part of Aberdeenshire had got a sergeant and twelve men, 'the County paying the men'.[129]

These are perfect examples of cooperation between county and army. The army was willing to lend soldiers and the county was willing to pay. Wherever possible, as in the case of a wealthy and populous county, the expense was usually borne by the commissioners, but where the expense would have been a burden the army paid. But payment in some cases was on a more subjective basis, being at the whim of the Duke of Cumberland as the supreme military commander for Scotland.

Eastwards of a line from Blairgowrie to Fort George the purely military origin and function of a road diminished, and there was more weight attached to its civil use. In this area there were some 250 miles of road designated as military: Fettercairn to Fochabers over the Cairn o' Mount, Stonehaven to Fochabers through Aberdeen, Portsoy to Huntly, Corgarff by Donside to Aberdeen, and parts of the Deeside road. Government interest in the area was such that, between 1772 and 1779, £6,500 was paid from military estimates for the bridge over the Deveron at Banff.[130]

Fettercairn to Fochabers

A route over the Cairn o' Mount, thence by Alford, Keith and Huntly to Fochabers existed long before Jacobitism, but the road was maintained by the army for a number of years, and the Cairn o' Mount sector was remade. The first official mention of this was in a letter from Churchill's aide to Caulfeild in 1752, proposing a road from Forfar, by Brechin, Fettercairn, Bridge of Dye and Kirk of Glentanar, to join the Braemar road near the old Kirk of Logie in Cromar. The road was 'already accessible for Wheel Carriages in summer, and can be made at a much less cost than by Cortachy, Clova and Loch Lee'. It is possible that this was an 'inspired leak' to let Caulfeild see how the general's mind was working, especially as he was at that time looking for a possible line.[131]

It is not clear when work started on this road, but the first mention of a military working party was in Lord Ligonier's Order Book for 1761, where work was recorded as going on in the Strathbogie sector, in the Fochabers area and at Cairn o' Mount itself. This is probably the time when the Cairn o' Mount was remade, because in 1763 a detachment of six NCOs and forty-eight men of the Suffolks repaired 4,485yd of this part of the road.[132] Two of the bigger bridges in this area had been in existence long before this—Whitestone Bridge over the Feugh, and Bridge of Dye, both built in 1681.

Between 1770 and 1780 the Cairn o' Mount to Strathbogie sector was regularly maintained at military expense at a total cost of almost £2,000. The stretch between Strathbogie, Keith and Fochabers was maintained until 1784 at a cost of almost £2,200.[133] In the 1790s, shortly after this road had been handed over to the counties, reports on its condition were favourable. This was partly due, no doubt, to the fact that the counties were given an allowance of £60 per annum for seven or eight years 'as an aid to put in good repair' the twenty miles between Fettercairn and Inchbear.[134] The ministers of Fettercairn and Strachan reported that road and bridges were in good condition, while the minister of Lumphanan emphasised that the counties were now responsible for road maintenance. From the parish of Birse came the news that Sir Alexander Ramsay had built a new five-arch bridge over the Feugh to replace the old Whitestone Bridge of 1681. The Dee, however, had still to be crossed by ferry. 'In no place is a bridge so much wanted as at Potarch . . . this road is much frequented and is used by the military . . . this very season [1793] the military had occasion to use this road, going north to quell the riots in Ross-shire; [again] in going from Fort George on account of the disturbances in Dundee.' Perhaps the final word should be the neat summing-up by the minister of Alford: 'Both of these roads since their foundation by the soldiery have been kept in repair by the statute labour of the parishes through which they pass.'[135]

A survey by the Commissioners of Highland Roads and Bridges revealed that 'the Cairn o' Mount road frequently rises not less than eight or nine inches in one yard, thereby becoming totally unfit for the purposes of civil life', and raised the question whether roads should be made over such gradients as Cairn o' Mount.[136] Probably posterity, fortified by the internal combustion engine, would answer in the affirmative.

Stonehaven to Fochabers and Portsoy

A road of sorts had existed between Stonehaven and Aberdeen since the Middle Ages, and a Highway Repair Act of 1686 put the roads and bridges in the care of the eight presbyteries of Aberdeenshire. The cost to heritors was ten shillings per £100 valued rent, while tenants were liable for six days a year of statute labour. Not much seems to have been achieved, because in 1716 Grant of Monymusk reported 'not one wheel carriage on [his] estate, nor indeed any one road that would allow it'. Another Road Act was passed in 1719, and a General Surveyor of Roads and Bridges in the county was appointed with a salary of 200 merks a year and sixpence a day travelling allowance.[137]

In 1756, in reply to a letter from Sir Arthur Forbes asking for military help in road making, General Bland replied that Cumberland and Colonel Watson had been discussing a better road from Aberdeen to Strathbogie 'whereby the Ferrys over the Done and Urey are avoided'. The new line would be by Fintry and Oldrain and the landowners would be expected to give such help 'as will enable one Serjeant and 20 men to make it practicable for Wheel carriages this season. The above number of troops whose labour will be paid by the Governm^{t}.' This was unusual generosity. On the same day Bland's secretary wrote to Caulfeild to send the usual tools for 'carrying on the road from Aberdeen to Strathbogie', so that Sir Arthur, his tenants and the soldiers could start work. Unfortunately there was a fortnight's delay when it was discovered that there were no tools in Aberdeen, which meant that they had to be sent from Leith.[138]

Tyrebagger Hill was always a problem on this road. Various routes were tried in the eighteenth century, including the part from Kinellar across the moor to Kintore. Among the roads repaired by a detachment of the 12th Foot in 1763 was a mile in this sector, including 3,670yd of drain. In addition the Stonehaven to Aberdeen part was repaired, and also 3,000yd over the 'Ben Hill'.[139] The fact that soldiers were employed on this road was enough for the Kinellar Muir part to be called 'General Wade's Road'. The Aberdeen to Strathbogie sector was repaired regularly between 1770 and 1774 at government expense at a cost of over £900. Thereafter there is no evidence of soldiers being employed. A Road Board minute of 1775 recorded that the Tyrebagger road was in a bad state of repair, and suggested that statute labour was inadequate and that military help should be sought, but there is no trace of a reply.[140] In 1784 General Mackay advised that this road should be handed over to the counties, which were 'well able to do so, and [have] for the most part done so, though it still stands on the list of military roads'.[141] There is no reason to doubt that this road was handed over to the counties in accordance with the general's recommendation.

Corgarff to Aberdeen

The pre-military road from Aberdeen to Aviemore went by Banchory, Kincardine O'Neil, Aboyne, Tarland, Kirk of Strathdon, Corgarff and the ford on the river Avon, according to a document of 1747. There was also the rather misleading advice that this route goes over a 'Hill called Leacht, which is not high, nor would it be difficult to carry the road over it'.[142]

In January 1754 General Bland wrote to Caulfeild in London asking him to recommend to Cumberland a request he had had from Grant of

Monymusk for a road from Aberdeen to Corgarff, where it would join the Coupar to Fort George road. He then continued:

> By allowing them a Serjeant and 12 Men next Summer to be paid at Governm[ts] Expence, the charge will be but trifling and I shall take care that they are employed to repair the worst Part of the Road, and that the Gentlemen who sign the Memorial shall be bound to give so many Labourers a Day at the Expence of the Country to work along with them; and that the Number of Country Labourers shall be specified to work with the Soldiers each day, and before the Party is sent.

Cumberland gave his blessing to the scheme without making it clear who was to pay the soldiers, because shortly afterwards Bland again wrote to Caulfeild asking for clarification. In subsequent years Bland continued to sponsor this road which keeps cropping up in correspondence until 1756 when, presumably, it was finished.[143]

The Deeside Road

For a full discussion of this road the reader is referred to *The Old Deeside Road* by G. M. Fraser. The road existed long before military building, but the part from Braemar to Balmoral was reconstructed as part of the road to Fort George. In a survey of the Braemar to Corgarff road made by Cadet Gunner Campbell, the Deeside road is marked as 'made by the Country People'.[144] Traces of an old road east of Balmoral are parts of the original civil road which, according to Keith in his *General View of the Agriculture of Aberdeenshire*, by 1798 the county was beginning to replace with a turnpike as part of a major reconstruction plan started in 1796.

CHAPTER 6

The Dumfries and Galloway Road

There is an obvious and natural tendency to associate any military road with the Highlands, and to attribute its origins directly to the need felt by the Hanoverian government to combat Jacobitism. There is, however, a stretch of road, over 100 miles long, which, geographically, could scarcely be farther away from the Highlands, which was not built to thwart the Jacobites, but which is, none the less, a military road. It runs between Bridge of Sark, near Gretna Green, and Port Patrick, with a northern arm from Stranraer to Ballantrae, and was built to facilitate the transport of troops to Ireland by the shortest route. There is abundant evidence to show that there were roads and bridges between Carlisle and Port Patrick long before the period of military activity. What did take place was a major reconstruction by the army with some realignment in the interests of easier communication. Most of this work was done between 1763 and 1765 by Major Rickson, Deputy Quartermaster-General in Scotland, under the overall supervision of Major Caulfeild.

The first practical step towards the Dumfries and Galloway road came from a joint meeting of the counties of Dumfries, Kirkcudbright and Wigtown on 14 September 1757, from which emanated an application to Lord George Beauclerk, the commander-in-chief, requesting that the 'Deputy Quarter Master General . . . may be ordered to survey and calculate the Expense of the Road from Sark Water to Port Patrick', adding that, 'they do one and all expect themselves to secure the assistance of the Troops and any further assistance in money from the Publick'. The response was virtually immediate. On

24 October of the same year, Major Rickson and Lieutenant Debbieg submitted a detailed survey and estimate. They noted that 'the intention of the proposed road is chiefly with a View to open a speedy, and certain communication between Great Britain and Ireland; especially with regard to the passage of Troops from one kingdom to the other whenever the exigency of Affairs may require it'. They surveyed two routes westward from Dumfries, one by New Galloway, the other by Gatehouse of Fleet, and were of the opinion that the latter was more suitable for both military and civilian purposes. Working on the principle of a road sixteen feet wide, they estimated a total cost of £2,130. The cost per mile varied according to the terrain: from the Sark to Gatehouse, £16 per mile; Gatehouse to Glenluce, £25 per mile; Glenluce to Port Patrick, £18 per mile. This did not include the cost and replacement of tools and was based on the assumption that troops would do the work at the usual rates. The concluding paragraph made it clear that the intention was to use the existing road with the necessary straightening and realignment.[1]

The minutes of the Commissioners of Supply for the Stewartry make it clear that there was a road in existence, but that it was not in a good state of repair, because in 1746 the judges on circuit complained about the state of the road and expected the commissioners 'would forthwith carry out the laws for repair of the Highways'. In 1748 the commissioners examined reports on the state of the roads, and established an order of priority for repairs, which they repeated with embellishments in 1759.[2] In the same year they drew up a scheme for the commutation of statute labour for a money payment, which formed the basis of an Act of Parliament in 1780. There were bridges over the main rivers, though some were in need of replacement.

Although the estimate and survey were made in 1757, there seems to have been no military work done until 1763. The report had established that much of the road from Bridge of Sark to Dumfries was good enough to be used without alteration. Five bridges would be needed, but the only major one was across the Sark. Road realignment was recommended in the areas of Gretna, Dornock, Ruthwell and Mouswald. Otherwise the existing road was to be used.

Work on the road westwards from Dumfries started in 1763 under control of Major Rickson, whose letters to John Dalrymple yr. of

Dunragit are a mine of information. In his first letter of 30 April 1763 Rickson referred to the difficulty of getting money in time, being 'obliged to give the Duke of Queensberry the trouble of speaking about it'. As Queensberry had estates bordering on the road, he had an obvious interest in 'speaking about it'. Rickson arrived in Dumfries on 30 May and made arrangements for quartering and rationing the 200 soldiers who were to be under his command.

The first contingent of 100 arrived on 9 June. Rickson decided to divide his work force into four sections, and to assign each 'to four stations', the first to the Bridge of Dee/Carlingwark area, the second between Anwoth and the Corse of Slakes, the third at Creetown and the fourth at Newton Stewart. The first party of three NCOs and thirty-six men was sent to the Bridge of Dee sector, 'the first bad piece of road after passing Carlingwark'. They were to work forward at first, then back towards Carlingwark. The second party was to work from Anwoth over the Corse of Slakes and also back towards Gatehouse. The third party, when it arrived, would work from Creetown to the Corse of Slakes, then back towards Newton Stewart. The fourth party would work from Newton Stewart to Creetown. The advantage of this scheme, Rickson felt, was that 'they can extend themselves both ways without change of quarters'.

Rickson was not happy about the bridges. He had sent two masons to examine river crossings but had not received a report from either.[3] One of the masons, Alexander Lawrie, had a contract from the commissioners for keeping in repair all the bridges in the Stewartry for twenty-one years for a fee of £36 a year. In fact, Lawrie had the contract until 1778.[4] Rickson indicated that because preliminary work had not been done on the bridges, he would have to confine himself for the present to any required by realignment from the existing road.

A strong plea had been made to take the road from Gatehouse to Creetown by the shore instead of by the existing road over the Corse of Slakes. Rickson rejected the proposal because it would have meant 'a considerable deviation . . . not in the plan already approved of'. He did, however, suggest other 'advantageous' alterations. The first was to 'strike off from the Dumfries road a quarter of a mile on this side [the Dumfries side] of the steps of Tarffe into the road leading to Kirkcudbright by Livingstone Boat; to have a bridge on the Tarffe between Underwood and Mr Maitland's at Barchapel and carry the road by the Kirk of Twynholm and near to Campbelltown to join the Kirkcudbright road from the Gatehouse and there come on the Hill of Enrig'. Although this would be a mile and a half longer, he felt that it would avoid many 'disadvantages' in the original survey. There was a road 'already almost the whole way', and 'there is not one pull, rock, moss or bad water all the way and the best of materials underfoot'. Another adjustment suggested was in the King's Laggan area of the Corse of Slakes road to avoid making a new bridge over the Skyre burn. A third proposal was for a different line from Graddock burn, outside Creetown, to Newton Stewart. The first two were carried out, but the third was found to be impracticable. Farther afield was a recommendation by Alexander Lawrie for a new bridge at Glenluce with an arch of 56ft.

Shortly afterwards Rickson went to Newton Stewart to discuss bridging with Lawrie because, until the site of bridges had been established, 'the direction of the road cannot be absolutely determined'. Lawrie and a Kirkcudbright mason, Kerr, submitted estimates for bridge widening at Carlingwark, a two-arch bridge at Kelton Mill, removing a bridge at Skyreburn, and bridges at Englishman's burn, Middle burn, Garrocher, and Monypoole. At £130 Lawrie was £40 cheaper than Kerr. Lawrie's estimate for all bridges between Dumfries and Port Patrick came to just over £600. Rickson decided that the best thing to do was to 'concentrate on the worst parts, finish them if possible, and join them up the following year'. To this end he detailed extra men to work on the Corse of Slakes.

In this letter Major Rickson gave useful information about the work rate expected of military parties. His Bridge of Dee and King's Laggan parties were good, but being 'used to task work they require very strict looking after in their day's work'. For this reason he put them to work 'at the same rate as Majr Caulfeild us'd to do, which was 1 yard and ½ a man for a day's work, and they sometimes do 2 yds and sometimes 2 yds and ½ in a day and the work equally well done. By this means their labour will be equal to one half of their number more. They go to work at 3 in the morn and leave off by twelve or one for the day.' The army has always been notorious for starting early, but a 3 am start meant being at work for an hour before even the miners of the time.

In the following year the men were doing two yards per man per day, but, he complained, 'I cannot yet prevail on them to do more than their task; they cou'd very well, but they don't like it. Many of them are Highlanders [Royal Scots Fusiliers]; but I will endeavour to lead them into it by encouraging small parties to do supernumerary work, for which I will give them ready money.' The carrot of overtime was to be dangled before their noses!

Rations were another of Major Rickson's worries. Before leaving the district in October 1763, he tried to make a deal about the supply of meal for the following year, but as no business could be done until the fiars prices were fixed, local dealers promised to contact him after 20 November. He had paid nearly £330 for meal in 1763, and felt that an early contract could be negotiated more cheaply. Having encountered the matter of fiars prices, Rickson then found himself embroiled in the lack of uniformity of weights and measures in Scotland. He was used to the Linlithgow stone of 14lb, and now found that the Galloway stone was 16lb. This meant that his contract in Dumfries for 1,000 Galloway stone of meal was 'almost a week's delivery gain'd by the difference of the weight of the Gallw. Lithgow weight'. His contractor offered to deliver as much as he required at eighteen pence for a 16lb stone. Rickson had to provide for 219 men for a sixteen-week period on the basis of an 8lb peck each per week, and an additional half peck per week for each of the forty female camp followers. He required 1,792 stone which, at £135, was a considerable saving on the previous year. Unfortunately, a week later, he found that the meal was 'North Country and very old . . . the men complain of it, so I do not find that we can deal with him'. Like Caulfeild he grudged the time lost at the beginning of the season, but agreed that they were 'early enough for the articles of provisions, which are extremely scarce and dear; not a bit of mutton or beef, only lamb and that is above twopence a pound'. Tents and huts were not required as the men were billeted on the local inhabitants. They 'board with their landlords at 22 pence a week and their meal, which tho' not very cheap is a convenient way and makes a good harmony between them, as it unites the soldier and landlord into one family'. There was, at least, a superficial cordiality between soldier and civilian, but Rickson was determined not to outstay his welcome. He meant to finish the Dumfries to Newton Stewart part of the road 'this summer, that the inhabitants may not be burthened a third season with the quartering of soldiers, which they do not consent to with good will'.

In October 1763 Major Rickson paid a visit to a Mr Graham of Netherby who had a complaint. He had supported the 'gentlemen of Scotland' when the road was proposed in 1756. Much of it had now been completed, but no one appeared to be doing anything about the twelve-mile stretch between the Sark and Carlisle, just because it was in England. He implied that if he was not assured of the support of his Scottish neighbours for this logical extension of the road, there might be difficulty about putting the Bridge of Sark on his land. Rickson smoothed the ruffled feathers to such an extent that Mr Graham not only agreed to the bridge, but promised active assistance.

With only three weeks of the season to go, Rickson gave a progress report:

> We have now finished the Corse of Slakes, which I could open in a couple of hours, but keep it shut . . . to prevent the cattle coming over it . . . and I hope the precautions we have taken against the waters will secure it. We have continued the communication from Palnure Burn to Graydock Burn and have another party working towards them from Creetown, but fear they will not be able to perfect a junction this season. I have a party working up the hill from Anwoth and tomorrow the Corse of Slakes party will begin a road to avoid the rockiest part of what is call'd the Haughs of Anwoth, working towards the other party . . . all the bad places between Newton Stewart and the Gatehouse are made good . . . I have proposed to Lord George [Beauclerk] to station 1 Serjt 1 Corpl and 12 men at the Gatehs as a party against smugglers who shall have instructions to visit all that district, particularly after tempestuous weather and to make up immediately any breaches that may be made.

He added that Lord Hillsborough had walked over the Corse of Slakes, was pleased with the job, and had given the men three guineas.

Work for the season finished on 22 October and Rickson recorded that the Corse of Slakes had been given a top dressing of slaty gravel. They had almost finished the road from 'the foot of the Path, toward the end of Barholme's territories'. The uncompleted part had been widened. The 'Hacks of Anwoth' had just been finished. 'We opened the road over the Corse two days ago and all friends are welcome. We only declare war against cattle and the Justices have refused them passports.'[5] The work done in 1763 was measured as follows: from the foot of the Path to beyond Graddock Bridge 5,015yd; from Graddock Bridge to Barholm's Croft, 2,112yd; from Englishman's Burn to beyond King's Laggan, 5,720yd; from Gatehouse to the Bush above the Cally, 1,107yd; from the march of Barncross to east of the Bridge of Dee, 2,301yd; giving a total of 16,255yd. In addition there were 7,571yd of back drain made, no fewer than 5,599 of them in the Corse of Slakes. Rickson had reported difficulty in the Corse with springs bubbling up through the road and hoped that the drains would end the trouble. In addition Lord George Beauclerk in his return to the War Office recorded that 520 rocks had been blown up and over 2,000yd of dry wall built.[6]

The following year the Royal Scots Fusiliers, stationed in Fort William, had to be reviewed in Stirling, and were not available until the end of June. There was also trouble about money from the banking firm of Coutts. However, Caulfeild seems to have paid a visit and arranged the finances. The first fifty men did not arrive until 7 July and were put to work from the bridge in Newton Stewart back towards the foot of the Path. They would then work from Barholm to Creetown, after which they would 'turn their faces towards Glenluce'. When the other parties arrived, they were put to work from Creetown to Englishman's Burn, from Anwoth to the Bridge of Fleet, and from Gatehouse to the Kirk of Twynholm. Then 'if we can manage more work this season we shall turn all the strength off towards Glenluce'.[7] Rickson described the NCOs as 'sober and attentive, some of them clever', the officers being 'very diligent in their attendance', and the men 'orderly and obedient'. By mid-July he hoped to be able to send at least one party to the Glenluce road in a few weeks. He had been told by Queensberry that a postal service was likely to be established between Dumfries and Port Patrick, which he hoped would be followed by one from Edinburgh to Dumfries, thus giving Edinburgh postal contact with Ireland.

By 1764 the military road from Dumfries to Newton Stewart followed the line, Lochfoot, Haugh of Urr, Carlingwark, the old road to Graniford (Rhonehouse), crossing the river at Graniford Bridge (Old Bridge of Dee), Ringford, Twynholm, over the hill past Littleton farm to Gatehouse, Anwoth Kirk, Corse of Slakes, Ferrytown of Cree to Cree Bridge. In 1772 the line was altered by the county onward from Rhonehouse. Instead of crossing by the Bridge of Dee, the road was carried on to old Tongland Bridge, crossing the Dee there, over the hill below Langbarns to Lower Tarff Bridge, then direct to Twynholm. In 1774 the commissioners for the Stewartry received a letter from Colonel Skene, Caufeild's successor, that 'a party of military were ordered by the Duke of Argyle to be sent this season for repairing the road betwixt Gatehouse of Fleet and Carlingwark not done last year', with a request for 'carriages to gravel the road properly'.[8] The government spent a lot of money on this road. Between 1765 and 1780 £2,000 was allotted every year, and from 1781 to 1785 £1,400 a year. Between 1765 and 1787 the total public expenditure was £41,230, with an additional £3,700 for the Stranraer to Ballantrae road. The total included repairs and maintenance of the harbour and lighthouse of Port Patrick.[9]

During the time when Sir Adolphus Oughton was commander-in-chief, twelve miles of road and twelve bridges were made between Stranraer and Ballantrae, through Glenap, during the years 1780–2. In each of these years the work was done by a party of two subalterns, six NCOs and sixty men working for the usual ninety-two-day period. In the following two years no new work was undertaken, but maintenance was carried out by two NCOs and twelve men. The cost of making this road was just under £2,900.[10]

General Mackay, commander-in-chief in 1784, believed that certain roads should be kept in repair by the counties rather than by the army.

> The first is the line of road from the Bridge of Sark . . . to Port Patrick . . . To this road is joined a small branch from Ballintrae in Ayrshire to Stranraer of 16 miles begun some years ago by Sir Adolphus Oughton for the purpose of shortening the distance in the marching of troops to Ireland . . . There are about five miles of this road yet unmade. This the gentlemen of the country offer to complete for the sum of £800 and to keep up that road in the future without any expense to the public. I would recommend the granting this sum . . . the demand is very moderate . . . the harbour of Port Patrick is completely in repair . . . the road from Bridge of Sark to Port Patrick will be in complete repair this season . . . the . . . Galloway roads should from this year cease to be a public charge.[11]

His proposal for the Ballantrae road was implemented, and in July

1790 the commissioners for Wigtownshire appointed a committee to 'mark out the line of Road from Stranraer to Cairn of Loch Ryan, Government having agreed to advance money for the same'. Mackay's main proposal, however, resulted in a compromise. East of the Bridge of Urr the county of Dumfries was made responsible for the road, but for the sixty-six miles from Bridge of Urr to Port Patrick, government assistance of £124 18s a year was given for maintenance. In July 1786 the commissioners for Wigtownshire received a letter from Major David Skene that '40 shillings sterling per mile was to be allowed by the Publick for keeping the road from the Watter of Orr to Stranraer, being Sixty Miles of which 26 are within this county'.[12]

In February 1786 Colonel Skene wrote to the commissioners for the Stewartry suggesting that they should complete the shore road from Creetown to Gatehouse, which was 'half made, as at that part of the county called the Corse of Slakes . . . the present military road is impassable in winter'. The commissioners agreed to this but decided to keep the Corse of Slakes under repair until the new road was made. In the following year the commissioners learned that a mail coach would soon start to run, going by Bridge of Tongland and the road which had been made in 1774, so they asked that the government grant should be applicable to this road rather than to the former military road by Graniford Bridge. In 1789 they took steps to put the 'Great Military Road' in order 'for the safe passage of the intended Mail Coach'. Finally in 1790 they expressed their obligation to the government for the provision of excellent packets between Port Patrick and Donaghadee, and 'of a Mail Coach seven times a week from Carlisle to Port Patrick'. In 1794 the commissioners felt it necessary to remind the 'Proprietors East of Urr' that the government grant was only for the road west of Bridge of Urr.[13] In 1795 the commissioners for Wigtownshire were told that most of the government money was spent on the section of the road between Tarf Bridge and Port Patrick, leaving very little for that between Cree Bridge and Tarf Bridge. The clerk was instructed to ensure that in future the proper proportion was allotted to both sections.[14]

Among information provided for the Finance Committee of the House of Commons were details of expenditure on the Galloway road: the maintenance grant of £124 1s 8d; the lighthouse at Port Patrick,

£32 12s 6d; repairs to the harbour at Port Patrick, £106 1s 3d; £112 10s 6d to the superintendent of military roads for salary and charges; more than £65 for tools. Including sundries the total was £510 0s 2d.[15]

The Stewarty Turnpike Act was passed in 1796 and was applicable to the road from Dumfries to Newton Stewart. Tolls were fixed and let by auction. In the same year Ainslie's map of the Stewartry was issued. In 1793 Ainslie had been instructed to make a map, 'showing levels', for £350. However, in 1795 the commissioners found that 'Mr Ainslie's map is in many respects defective and erroneous and instruct him to stop engrossing the map until the errors are rectified'. Two years later the revised map was accepted.[16]

In correspondence with the Treasury in 1798–9 General Abercrombie pointed out that, whatever happened to the military roads, the pier and lighthouse required separate treatment. He also warned that 'if government do give up military roads they will have to compensate the Overseers' and many others. For the years 1795–7 the cost to the government for maintenance of the Galloway road was £372, and for the pier and lighthouse £274. Eventually the sixty-six miles between Bridge of Urr and Port Patrick were handed over in 1805, when payments were stopped, but the pier and lighthouse remained on public charge.[17] On 30 April 1806 the balance of the military road fund, amounting to £155, was handed over to the Road Trustees for the Stewartry.[18] In Wigtownshire the government seems to have been unusually generous. On 13 April 1807 the commissioners handed over, not only the balance of the military road fund, £13 15s 4d, but also an additional £60 2s 9d 'received from Government in 1806'.[19] So it was that the last tenuous connection with the old military road system came to a quiet and peaceful end.

CHAPTER 7

The Final Phase

With the passage of time, and with Jacobitism becoming more and more a romantic memory rather than a potential danger, the government began to regard the military roads as something of a penitential albatross around its neck, and sought ways and means of relieving itself of the burden. The death of William Caulfeild in 1767 seemed a good opportunity for reappraisal. The Treasury reluctantly gave Colonel Skene, Caulfeild's successor, the £6,867 which he estimated for the roads, but warned him that in future they might not 'think themselves sufficiently authorised to make any further issues'. They then called in the Marquis of Lorne, who was commander-in-chief, and Colonel Skene for interrogation. Skene left them in no doubt that 'when the whole of the military roads—which will consist of 997 miles, of which 139 are yet unfinished—are completed, it will require about £6,000 per annum to keep the said roads and 815 bridges in repair'. This placed their lordships in an awkward position from which they extricated themselves by replying that because of the lateness of the application for road money, the only course open to them was to grant Skene the sum requested, after which they asked the commander-in-chief to indicate 'what part of the roads in the Highlands he is of opinion may be maintained by toll'.[1] The suggestion of tolls in the Highlands at this time displayed an ignorance of the situation in the north which was not unique in Treasury circles. Lorne tactlessly on the same day presented a petition for bridges over the Beauly and Conon. The petition was rejected, 'as it proposes the undertaking of a new road'. While the Treasury, with reluctance, maintained its responsibility for existing roads, it was not prepared to sanction any new work.

A minor controversy arose over the annual grant for repair of

General Wade's roads, which were now regarded as the 'old roads'. This money had been paid out of the military contingent fund, and then agreed by Parliament. In 1769 it was decided that the cost should be met from receipts of exchequer. From 1770 until 1784 detailed annual estimates were laid before Parliament, but this did not lead to reduced expenditure. During these fifteen years the total exceeded that of the previous fifteen years by £6,400.[2]

In September 1784 the Lords of the Treasury, activated by the fact that since 1770 parliamentary grants for the military roads had averaged £7,000 a year, asked General Mackay to report on how they might be repaired with greater saving to the public.[3] The general replied at length. 'A line,' he felt, 'should be drawn where the county is capable of keeping them in repair by the statute labour, and where, from the wildness and barrenness of the country and the small number of inhabitants, the expense must unavoidably be defrayed by the public.' There were by this time about 1,100 miles of road listed as military, and the general went on to explain that the demarcation line would need to be drawn with 'care and propriety'. There were some roads which, he was 'clearly of opinion', might now be 'kept in repair by the county'. First was the Dumfries and Galloway road. Turning to the north-east he indicated that the road from Stonehaven by Aberdeen to Portsoy and Fochabers could be handed over to be repaired by the county, which 'has for the most part done so, though it still stands on the list of military roads'. These were his immediate proposals.

To cut costs the general suggested repairs done by contract. The inspector should have a sum placed to his credit to be drawn on a warrant by the commanding officer. He should have a fixed sum embracing salary, expenses and payment of a clerk. He should also have the services of a qualified bridge overseer. The roads, unfortunately, were in a bad state of repair, 'from want of troops . . . with which I could not supply him from the small numbers we have had'. With the changing political situation permitting a reduction of the military establishment, the shortage of soldier labour was acute, and was a factor necessitating change. Mackay concluded by suggesting that the roads should be classified and divided into districts.[4]

During 1785 Major Fraser, an engineer, made a detailed survey of the military roads which the general summarised for the Treasury.

There were 682 miles of military road in the Highlands, mostly in a bad state of repair and in some cases impassable for carriages. There were 938 bridges or 1,031 arches, many of which were 'insufficient, ruinous and ill executed'. Repair and construction of bulwarks, embankments and retaining walls was necessary. It would require an expenditure of £4 per mile and £2 per bridge 'for some years' to put roads and bridges in good shape, apart from 'fifty major bridges which would have to be dealt with separately'. Bulwarks, embankments and walls would need £300 a year to be kept in good repair. He warned that this did not take account of snow and rain damage. 'Last year a thunderstorm happened which in a few hours carried off fifteen bridges, damaged twelve others, and rendered five miles of road impassable.' He advised nine pieces of realignment at a cost of £1,268, which the general endorsed. The tenth was the last stage of the Stirling to Fort William road, where

> the road was conducted over so steep a range of hills that it is impassable for carriages, incapable of improvement, and kept even in its present state at a great expense. He proposed a new line of road, a considerable part of which is already made by the country. The commissioners of annexed estates . . . gave £500 towards it . . . estimate the compleating at £780.

This meant abandoning the Devil's Staircase and the Lairig Mòr, in favour of Glencoe, Ballachulish ferry and Onich. The estimate for all the necessary repairs to roads and bridges, a salary of £100 for a bridge surveyor, and the Glencoe diversion was £5,784.[5] Mackay added that although this seemed a high price, he was 'perfectly satisfied that the sums mentioned are absolutely necessary . . . for some years'. With the important exception of contract work, General Mackay's proposals were adopted, and in 1787 Major Fraser received £134 14s 7d for his work.[6]

This meant an end to the distinction between Wade's 'old roads' and the post-Wade roads, and the £500 repair allowance became the inspector's salary. From this time there was a steady running down of military working parties. By 1789 the extra pay for soldiers had dropped to £142 10s 6d. Thereafter soldiers were no longer used and so a long, adventurous and interesting era came to an end.

The discrepancy of about 400 miles between 1768 and 1785 is accounted for by the handing over of the Dumfries and Galloway road and the north-east roads, and the disregarding of the Contin to Poolewe road. In 1790 the inspector, Hugh Montgomerie, recommended handing over the road from Dumbarton to Crieff by way of Stirling. Shortly after this the Bridge of Allan to Callendar road was handed over. By this time the annual expenditure on military roads was averaging £4,700, and remained at this figure until 1803. The government, however, wanted to put these roads on the charge of local funds, and the select committee on finance in 1798 asked for a 'more minute detail' of expenditure. The accounts of the new inspector, Sir Charles Preston, were presented. £1,600 had been spent on the roads, £2,139 on bridges, £124 to the Galloway lairds for upkeep, and £200 for the harbour and lighthouse at Port Patrick. With salaries and fees the total spent was £5,575 13s 9d.

In November 1798 the Treasury asked the new commander-in-chief if he thought 'the Grant may be immediately discontinued' and again asked for detailed accounts over the past three years. Abercrombie replied that from the military angle the roads and fortifications had outlived their usefulness, but added a plea for the retention of the roads, not just as a civil amenity, but as a necessity. The roads for which he was responsible

consist of 599 miles, and about one thousand bridges. All these Roads pass through districts of country very poor and thinly inhabited, and totally unable to keep in repair either the Roads or Bridges; and if Government withdraw the usual aid, many of the Roads will be rendered impassable in a winter or two, and the whole of them in a few years ... The Military Roads may be divided into Three principal lines, and Six Cross Roads; viz.

1st Line
From Callender, by Lochearnhead to Tyndrom, and from Luss, by Tarbet, Inveraray, Dalmallie, Tyndrom, Blacksmount, Glenco, Ballichulish Ferry, Fort William, Fort Augustus, Inverness, Fort George
212 Miles   295 Bridges

2nd Line
From Inverness by Dalmagarrie, Aviemore, Pitmain, Dalwhinnie, Dalnacardoch, Blair, Dunkeld and Ambelrie to Crieff
120 Miles   270 Bridges

3rd Line
From Fort George by Dulsie Bridge, Grantoun and Braemar to Cupar
112 Miles   128 Bridges

1st Cross Road
From Tarbet through Glenfalloch to Tyndrom
16 Miles   58 Bridges

2nd Cross Road
Fort Augustus to Bernera
43 Miles   41 Bridges

3rd Cross Road
Fort Augustus over Corriarick to Dalwhinnie
31 Miles   12 Bridges

4th Cross Road
Dulsie Bridge by Lochindorb to Aviemore
20 Miles   19 Bridges

5th Cross Road
Aviemore to Grantoun
13 Miles   9 Bridges

6th Cross Road
Dalnacardoch by Tay Bridge to Ambelrie
32 Miles   98 Bridges

The total was 599 miles and 930 bridges, all in reasonable repair.
Abercrombie ended his report with the detailed expenditure for the
past three years. The total was almost £14,000. The roads and bridges
each cost over £5,000, the remainder being incidentals.

In 1799 Colonel Anstruther, the inspector, submitted a memorial
which Abercrombie submitted to the Treasury. After a historical
justification of the military roads he continued:

> That the Highlanders are disposed to be industrious, and will pursue it with
> avidity when they meet with encouragement, appears from the progress in
> making the fisheries, and the linen and cotton manufactures . . . and for the
> carrying on of which Roads are absolutely necessary. If the government stop
> maintaining these roads the Highlanders will in a few years relapse into their
> former ignorance or desert their country.

Roads should be handed over only when population and industry
justified it. The payments for roads, pier and lighthouse in Galloway
could easily be stopped, thus saving £300 a year. The only other road
he could recommend giving up was between Blairgowrie and Coupar
Angus, a distance of three miles![7] Anstruther made it clear that as the
military roads were the only form of communication in the Highlands,

they must remain, and that to deprive the Highlanders of their only roads would be a disaster. Luckily he was not alone in his opinion.

Asked in 1807 what roads had been handed over recently, Anstruther replied that eighty-five miles had been cut down, but that 'forty three miles [Fort Augustus to Bernera] never existed as a road'. This, of course, was untrue; but at least the non-existent road was formally struck off the list. Of the remaining forty-two miles, 'one portion was only proposed to be abandoned', another was 'never out of the estimate', while the part from Callendar to Lochearnhead was 'replaced on the List in 1810, by order of the Lords of the Treasury'. After this the inspector gave up trying to hand over roads and the extent remained at approximately 530 miles.

In 1801 and 1802 the government instructed Thomas Telford to make a survey of the Highlands. Among those interviewed by Telford was the Highland and Agricultural Society. The Society shared his and the government's belated alarm at the depopulation of the Highlands, which they blamed in part on the landowners' overstocking with sheep, and they all felt that the provision of roads, bridges, canals and harbours would be a prerequisite to prosperity. The Highland Society were of the opinion that 'even the lines of Communication by means of Military Roads, in some parts of the Highlands, have been productive of Benefit to the Country'.

After examining Telford's report a committee of Parliament recommended that the government should pay half of the expense of what roads and bridges were deemed necessary. The other half was to be met by landlords and others who might benefit. Provision should be made for proper repairs, and commissioners should be appointed to see that the roads were made with 'prudence and economy'.[8] The result was the Highland Road and Bridge Act of 1803, based on the committee's proposals, with the amazing omission of any provision for repairs. There also came into being the Commissioners for Highland Roads and Bridges, to administer this and subsequent Acts. It had been proved time and again that without regular maintenance Highland roads deteriorated rapidly, and this was true of the new 'parliamentary roads'.

A new Act was passed in 1810 empowering the counties to assess themselves for the repair of roads made under the 1803 Act, and allowing any heritor in the county, or any five heritors in another county, who could prove that such a tax was not being levied, to have it enforced by the sheriff or the Court of Session.[9] The experiment of trying to get the landowners to assess themselves was a failure, and no heritor exercised his powers under the Act. The commissioners discovered, with alarm, that 'the Roads first finished [are] now evidently falling to decay'. It was obvious that action would have to be taken, and that public aid would be necessary. As it would be absurd to have two authorities for Highland roads, it would be logical to include the military roads in any new scheme. This prompted the Commons to ask a number of questions on the military roads in 1813 to help them to frame an Act embracing military and parliamentary roads.

The Commons asked first of all for information about the Inspector of Roads. Colonel Anstruther produced his commission as inspector, but declared that there was nothing at all about his duties, except that he must do and perform 'all manner of things thereunto belonging' and that he was under the commander-in-chief. As for travel and expenses, he wrote, 'The present Inspector ... has travelled annually ... from 900 to 1,000 miles, and never had any allowance whatever for travelling expenses.' He then submitted the rules which he had drawn up for his superintendent: to survey the roads and bridges at the end of the season so that the inspector could make his estimates; to get certificates from the Justices of the Peace of daily rates of wages to enable the inspector to check the overseer's returns; to check charges with certificates of wages; to check names and numbers; to see that workers were 'worthy of the wages charged for them, in youth, skill and strength'; to check horses and carts; to report improper conduct, negligence or carelessness; to check tools; to order emergency repairs caused by winter floods.

Parliament also wanted to know what roads had been abandoned since 1798, and why some had been returned. The total was forty-seven miles and forty-three bridges. Thirty-one miles and twenty-seven bridges had been returned, leaving only sixteen miles and sixteen bridges given up. The list had been approved by the Treasury in 1805 and the same letter had stopped payment for the Galloway road. The Inverness to Dores road had been taken back because it was illogical to have eight miles of a main road under a different authority. The Inverness to Fort George road was restored because the county had failed to make another road and the governor complained about lack of access. The Callendar to Lochearnhead road was rather sheepishly restored after a long and spirited correspondence between Sir John Murray of Lanrick and the Treasury. He pointed out that the area was thinly populated, with only two shepherds for many miles, and also that the weavers and tradesmen of Doune, unskilled in road making, were not obliged to go beyond four miles of Doune in performance of statute labour. The Treasury capitulated and the road was returned to the military list in 1810 after repairs costing £738.

Parliament finally asked what new roads and alterations had been made since 1798. From the reply it was obvious that Mackay's proposed reforms had been implemented, the roads and bridges having been divided into districts under overseers. There followed a list of all the alterations between 1798 and 1813 in miles and yards, the size of bridges, the cost, and why the alterations had been done. There had been fifty-three miles of alterations and forty-eight bridges made at a cost of £22,699. To this was added £247 1s 7d in 1810 for making the last military road in Scotland, 927yd long, being a 'footpath from the Town of Perth to the Depot for Prisoners of War'.[10] (Details of the alterations during this period are in Part Two, below.) Finally Colonel Anstruther gave the expenditure from 1798 to 1813:

	£	s	d
Roads made 54 miles	15,575	7	7
Bridges built or rebuilt 79	11,094	12	1
Bridges & Bulwarks repaired	17,631	19	9
Roads repaired	21,473	12	3
	£65,775	11	8

To this had to be added a further £18,000 for salaries and incidentals, giving a final total of £83,774 6s 6d. All this was analysed by the Treasury and the Commissioners for Highland Roads and Bridges. Military road mileage was accepted as 530, distributed among the Highland counties as follows: Perth, 148 miles; Argyll, 77; Inverness, 181; Elgin, 41; Aberdeen, 37; Dunbarton, 20; Nairn, 16; Banff, 10.

Based on figures for the past sixteen years the annual cost of keeping the roads and bridges in repair was £5 per mile, compared with £4 for the parliamentary roads. On the supposition that each county would pay three-quarters of the cost of repairing both military and parliamentary roads, and using the 1811 rental as a basis, the counties would be required to assess themselves as follows:

	Miles	Cost (£)	Rate per £1
Inverness	524	2,277	2½d
Argyll	209	913	⅞d
Perth	148	740	$\frac{3}{11}$d
Ross	139	556	1⅛d
Elgin	41	205	$\frac{6}{10}$d
Aberdeen	37	185	⅛d
Nairn	28	128	2d
Dunbarton	20	100	$\frac{3}{10}$d
Banff	10	50	⅛d

The commissioners condemned as inefficient the existing system of 16 overseers and 270 men working for 100 days in summer, and recommended, as General Mackay had done, that the work should be put to contract.[11]

If the counties paid three-quarters, the government would pay only £1,500 of the £6,000 for repairs. It would also pay the £2,000 for salaries and incidentals. Should there be any alteration in the line of military roads in future, a 'moiety of the expense' should be borne by those most likely to benefit. If the counties decided that there was no longer any need for a military road, it would be abandoned. Separate provision would be made for large bridges. The inspector should have access to gravel. This was necessary because some landowners had taken legal action against him for removing gravel from their land.

The southern parts of Perthshire objected strongly to the proposed payment of three-quarters, because everyone coming from farther north had to use their roads. When the point was made that military roads were of no use for local purposes, the commissioners drew attention to the fact that Perthshire had received £4,000 of public money since 1803 for altering the military road at Blairgowrie. The Highland Society, which favoured a general county assessment for road repairs rather than an assessment only on the district through which the road passed, expressed the opinion that 'by the conveyance of these roads, the south receives annually a great supply of sheep, cattel, wool, and other articles from the northern and Highland districts'. In general the Society deplored any intention to give up the military roads, pointing out that they had to be used by the judges on circuit. There were too few people to use statute labour and tolls would bring in very little. The Society felt strongly that the military roads were of greater national than local importance. These opinions were strongly supported by the county of Inverness.

The result of all the activity was the 1814 Act 'for maintaining and keeping in repair certain Roads and Bridges in Scotland, for the purpose of Military Communication and for making more effectual Provisions for maintaining and repairing Roads made and Bridges built under the authority of the Parliamentary Commissioners for Highland Roads and Bridges'.[12] With some additions the 1803 commissioners were appointed to administer the 'Road Repair Act'. All roads were to be maintained at public expense for the first year. Thereafter the expense was borne as discussed above. To avoid undue hardship in some counties the assessment was limited to three-half pence in the pound of rental. The Act was compulsory for the parliamentary roads, but only to such military roads as the counties were prepared to hand over to the commissioners. The Act achieved the sensible purpose of putting all the Highland roads under one authority, the Commissioners for Highland Roads and Bridges; but to saddle the counties with a major share in the expense of maintenance of roads still designated 'for Military Communication' was, perhaps, less sensible. It is debatable whether or not roads should be a national or a local charge, but there should be no doubt in the case of roads which, even in 1814, were called 'military'.

Inverness-shire, Morayshire and Argyllshire took advantage of the optional clause for handing over their military roads. Perthshire and Dunbartonshire opted out with disastrous consequences for future travellers. Inverness handed over the Badenoch road as far as Drumochter, the Boleskine road (Loch Ness), Corrieyairack road, Fort George and Fort William roads. Morayshire handed over the Grantown road and the Duthel road. Argyllshire handed over the Dalmally road (Tyndrum to Inveraray), Tyndrum to Ballachulish, and Inveraray to Loch Long. This amounted to 283 miles.

In reports of 1816–17 the commissioners said that the Inverness-shire military roads had been repaired and the annual cost would be £7 4s per mile. The Argyllshire roads being in a bad state cost £11 16s per mile. The Morayshire roads were just over £11 per mile. The total cost for all military roads in this year was £2,618 1s 11d, giving an average of just over £9 0s per mile. The comparatively new parliamentary roads cost £4 0s per mile.[13]

In 1819 the commissioners reported that their funds were insufficient. As this would preclude any future realignment, Parliament repealed and replaced the 1814 Act.[14] The counties still had to find three-quarters of the cost, but their assessment was not to exceed a penny in the pound. The Treasury would find £5,000 a year, and any expense in excess would be borne equally by the Treasury and the counties. There were complaints from both sides. In the midst of the controversy Perthshire was overtaken by slow-footed justice. In 1820 the Perth-shire Military Road Act decreed that the road from Dunkeld to Drumochter must always be maintained in as good a state as the Badenoch road.[15]

Between 1803 and 1816 over £450,000 had been spent on the making of Highland roads and bridges, including over £50,000 from the funds of the forfeited estates.[16] This was 875 miles of road and several large bridges. To help to meet the increasing expenditure, the 1823 Toll Gate Act was passed.[17] It applied to the counties of Inverness, Sutherland, Caithness and Ross, and gave the heritors three options. They could increase the assessment as each year required; they could erect toll gates to assist the assessment; or they could erect toll gates in lieu of assessment.

With the coming of turnpikes and stage-coaches there was no longer any distinction between types of roads, but until the end of their tenure in 1863 the commissioners officially used the term 'military roads'. These roads, crossed by toll gates, and running alongside the new railways, justified and would surely have gratified General Wade as the father of Highland communications.

In their final report in 1863 the commissioners recalled that 930 miles of parliamentary roads had been built at a cost of £540,000, and that after 1814 the addition of 255 miles of military roads had given them nearly 1,200 miles under their care. An Act of Parliament instructed them to maintain their roads until the end of 1862, after which they should be handed over to the counties.[18] In their final report the commissioners wrote:

> In resigning the trust which they have had the honour of executing for a period of sixty years, they cannot but look back with satisfaction . . . they have watched with the greatest interest the improvement of the country which it was the beneficent design of Parliament to civilise and enrich. They found it barren and uncultivated—inhabited by heritors without capital or enterprise, and by a poor and ill-employed peasantry—and destitute of trade, shipping and manufactures. They leave it with wealthy proprietors, a profitable agriculture, a thriving population, and active industry. The value of the land has been incalculably increased, and the condition of every class of the people improved . . . The Highlands, whence a scanty revenue was formerly drawn, now furnish their fair proportion of taxes to the national exchequer.[19]

It is a report in which justifiable pride of achievement jostles with bland assumptions derived from over-simplified generalisations. Perhaps because of the nature of their preoccupations, they were prepared to equate progress with the growth of material prosperity, without looking too closely at the inequalities inherent in Highland society during this period. Their criterion was the annual amount paid in taxation to the national exchequer. They appear to have been totally unaware that the outward prosperity of these years was punctuated by the Clearances, and by the slow death of a language, a culture and a way of life which had been struck a mortal blow on Culloden Moor.

Conclusion

The military roads, born of strategic necessity in an age when political revolution was not only a threat but a reality, were the fundamentally important first stage in the development of Highland communications. Apart from the Dumfries and Galloway road, which was built for the passage of troops through Scotland to Ireland by the shortest route, all the other military roads were constructed or maintained to facilitate the movement of troops within Scotland, north of a line from Dumbarton, through Stirling, to Perth. In any assessment of the military roads it is important never to lose sight of the fact that they were built primarily for the movement of troops and their equipment. They invariably followed traditional route lines, but in local alignment and gradient they were geared to military rather than civilian requirements. In the eyes of posterity the military roads have always been compared unfavourably with Telford's roads. In many ways this is an unfair comparison, because posterity tends to ignore the fact that Thomas Telford's brief was very different from that given to George Wade and William Caulfeild. The lumbering stage-coach of the nineteenth century found difficulty in coping with parts of the military roads, for which the military engineers were unjustly blamed. Seldom is a voice of criticism raised against Telford, whose roads are equally inadequate for coping with twentieth-century requirements. One of the most interesting features of twentieth-century road development in the Highlands, and with particular reference to the proposals for the virtual supersession of the present A9 road between Dunkeld and Inverness, is that some of the suggested realignment is approximating to and coinciding with the line of the original military road. It is obvious that the Drumochter route is far from being the only practicable line of communication between north and south, yet there has never been a serious attempt to supplant General Wade's choice. The same may be said for the other major military routes.

The main criticism levelled at the military roads has been that they were unsuitable for civilian purposes. However true this may have been in some respects, and in many ways the faults have been exaggerated by those who had their own good reasons for so doing, the fact remains that they were properly engineered roads, and there is every reason to believe that if Wade and Caulfeild had been required to design roads for civilian purposes, they would not have been lacking in the necessary skills to produce a different pattern.

In the earlier period of their existence the military roads were regarded with mixed feelings by the inhabitants of the Highlands. Associated with a distant and alien government, they enabled agents of that government to move in the central Highlands with disconcerting and unprecedented freedom. Before the '45 this simple fact was hated by many as an unwarrantable encroachment on previously enjoyed privacy. The Highlanders themselves, having found the lack of roads little impediment to their general mobility, argued in consequence that the new roads must be purely for the benefit of incomers and intruders. There were those among them who would follow the line taken by the road, as it was the route they were wont to use, but who would not set foot on the road itself, and who, to show their independence of manufactured travellers' aids, would wade through the rivers rather than use the bridges. Such people, of course, were extremists, and in time their number diminished. That the roads were invaluable for troop movement, the purpose for which they were built, requires no proof. During the '45 General Wade's roads were useful to both sides. One general made the criticism that they were vulnerable to attack. This is perfectly true, but can scarcely be regarded as a criticism of the *roads*. The vulnerability was a geographical phenomenon which forced troops to use particular routes. Indeed, a military road through an already vulnerable pass could be a positive advantage, as the troops could move along it more quickly. Leaving military considerations aside, however, there was certainly no enthusiasm for the Wade roads among the indigenous population. When not viewed with antipathy, they were accepted with apathy

The later roads had one feature in common with Fort George. They saw no shots fired in anger. They were inevitably associated with the repressive measures which followed the '45, and were undoubtedly one of the factors contributing to the ending of the traditional life and culture of the Highlands. In the climate of the times they were regarded by the Hanoverian government as a necessary insurance policy against a possible resurgence of Jacobitism. This second phase of military road building opened up the Highlands as never before, at a time when the old way of life of a rudely mauled populace was particularly vulnerable to external influences, whether material or cultural. It would be an exaggeration to blame the military roads alone for the break-up of Highland life. There were many government-inspired contributory factors, of which the roads, as practical and symbolic reminders of the army of occupation, certainly played their part. Highlanders, particularly the generations which knew Jacobitism, can scarcely have regarded these probing tentacles of governmental control with feelings of equanimity, far less of approbation. As the fear of Jacobitism receded, the Highland garrisons were steadily run down, and long before the end of the eighteenth century they had either become token forces or disappeared completely. The result was that the roads were used less and less by the soldiery, and more and more by civilian traffic. It was this increasing civilian use which gave rise, more than anything, to criticism of the roads on the grounds of unsuitability for a purpose for which they had never been designed.

Towards the end of the eighteenth century there was considerable pressure from some in high places to abandon roads which were no longer required for military purposes. In more populous areas the roads were handed over to the county authorities to maintain, but it was realised that, in sparsely populated parts, this would impose an intolerable burden. While successive governments, with increasing reluctance, continued to pay for the upkeep of the military roads, it is to their credit that they did not abandon assets which had been built with so much skill and labour. Not only were the roads maintained, but they were progressively realigned in the interests of easier travel, until in the nineteenth century they were ultimately absorbed into the Highland communication system which embraced Telford's parliamentary roads, the Caledonian Canal and the railways.

As intruments of governmental control in an area regarded as remote and barbarous by most people in London and by some even in Edinburgh, the military roads admirably served the purpose for which they had been instituted. From a technical point of view, and within the context of strategic requirements, they were realistically conceived and skilfully executed. During the period of military occupation there was never any lack of manpower, not only to build, but also to maintain the roads in a fit state for use by the army and others who chose to visit the Highlands. That the state of maintenance was generally good is evident from accounts given by most of those who had occasion to travel on them, and who frequently compared them favourably with roads in other parts of the country. The traverses, buttresses and bulwarks of the Corrieyairack, of Rest and Be Thankful and of Trinafour are works of which any civil engineer would be justifiably proud. The long straights above Bohespic, across Cochrage Moor or leading up to the Corrieyairack have about them an arrow-like directness reminiscent of the Roman road. The bridges over Tay, Tummel, Garry, Spey at Garbhamòr, Spean, and Findhorn at Dulsie, have a romantic grace and beauty which almost belie their usefulness and efficiency. Although considerations of natural beauty were far from the minds of the military road makers, there can surely never have been, apart from the Caledonian Canal and the Highland Railways, a more scenic communication system.

Despite claims made, modestly by General Wade, and more immoderately by the Commissioners for Highland Roads and Bridges, the military roads made little economic impact on the Highlands, at least not until the nineteenth century, by which time they had become part of a more general communication system. In reply to a series of questions posed by Telford in 1802, the Highland Society of Scotland replied that

> even the Lines of Communication by Means of Military Roads, in some parts of the Highlands, have been productive of Benefit to the Country, though the Motives which gave rise to their Formation, having no Relation to Objects of Commerce or Industry, the Advantages derived from them are very imperfect and the Want of further Roads has been the greatest Obstacle to the Introduction of useful Industry.[1]

In the days when they were the only roads in the Highlands, the all-important cattle trade had no real use for them. The old grassy tracks were far more suitable for both man and beast. Nevertheless, whatever derogatory remarks have been made on the military roads by Telford and others before and since, it should be remembered that, although they were built, not for the benefit of the local inhabitants, but as strategic arteries for use by an army of occupation in controlling the region, they did give the Highlands a communication system before there were many 'made roads' in the Lowlands. In this respect the military roads efficiently achieved their primary purpose, but they must always be regarded with mixed feelings by the Highlanders themselves, because in opening what had been a closed book, they made their own contribution to the disintegration of Highland life and culture.

PART TWO

The Roads Today

The Roads Today

Map references are given in this form: 35/41/131762. The first pair of digits, 35, refers to the sheet number of the existing one-inch maps. The second pair of digits, 41, refers to the sheet number of the 1:50,000 maps to be introduced in 1976. In either case the six-figure map reference remains the same.

In the sketch maps which accompany the text, the thick black line indicates the military road, either on its own or with the modern road superimposed. The broken line indicates a modern road. The scale throughout is rather less than 1 inch : 1 mile.

Where bridges are not marked, the original river crossings were by ferry or ford.

Fort William to Inverness (Great Glen Road)

Fort William, at the southern terminal of the road, has been so cannibalised that there is little to be said on the subject now. The seaward wall remains, but the ground on which the fort stood was used as a railway yard, and there is now little trace of anything else. The main gateway of the fort has been removed and is now the entrance to the cemetery.

The road left Fort William on much the same line as at present, crossing the Nevis, and continuing until about a quarter of a mile beyond the second milestone, at 35/41/131762, where there is a lay-by. Through the gate it can be seen in the field, then skirting the river side of the wood, it passes in front of Inverlochy Castle to Torlundy. It crosses the present road, over the railway bridge, past the forestry office and alongside the wood for about two miles before crossing the railway to the A82 near the sixth milestone at 36/41/169790. It then crossed to the left of the present road, and although cultivation has removed all trace at 36/41/176795, there is a very distinct track from 36/41/179803 making straight for the High Bridge. This fine bridge, which saw the first action of the '45, is now, unfortunately, in ruins, but the road can easily be picked up on the other side of the Spean, running parallel to the river for just over half a mile and coming up to the B8004 at 36/41/198831 about 200yd from a quarry at the sharp corner. It then makes off to the right, to spot height 427, where it swings off by the pylons to the AA Box at Stronenaba (Map 2). Here it crosses the A82, runs along the side of a field, and comes down again at Rathliesbeag, 36/41/210852. It follows the present road for rather more than a mile to the sign post to Glen Gloy, before crossing the river Gloy by the Low Bridge, or Nine Mile Bridge, after which it follows a well-defined track to the former Invergloy station, 36/41/230887. From this point to Letterfinlay it may have been either on the line of the old railway or that of the present road. A short stretch can be seen going off to the left among the trees at 36/34/280949, coming up again at 36/34/284955. Just before the Laggan swing bridge it breaks off to the right at 36/34/299983 through the disused station yard and, running parallel to the former railway, it hugs the east shore of Loch Oich, coming up by Calder Cottage, and rejoining the main road at Aberchalder, 36/34/342035 (Map 3). From here to Fort Augustus it follows the line of the A82, though there are traces of an earlier road up to the right.

Between Fort William and Fort Augustus the High Bridge is certainly worth a visit; the road from Low Bridge to Invergloy is a pleasant mile or so, and the road alongside Loch Oich from Laggan to Aberchalder is a rewarding walk of about four miles. Wade's Fort Augustus is now, of course, the Benedictine Abbey, and a loopholed wall of the original fort can be seen behind the Lovat Arms Hotel (Map 4).

From Fort Augustus the road skirts the end of Loch Ness before climbing up to Glendoe. There are several minor deviations from the present road up to Loch Tarff, and at 36/34/407088 an old bridge over the Allt Doe can be seen down to the left. There are other minor deviations between here and White Bridge. The old bridge is still

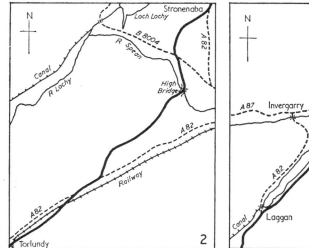

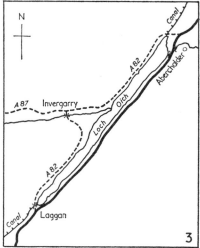

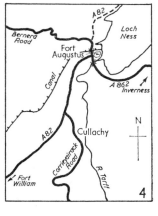

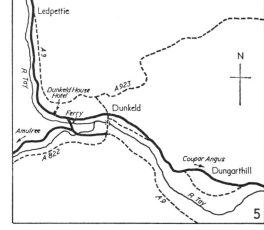

2 High Bridge area; 3 Loch Oich area; 4 Fort Augustus area: this map illustrates the importance of Fort Augustus as a communication centre, showing the convergence of the roads from Bernera, Fort William, Inverness and Dalwhinnie; 5 Dunkeld area: junction of the roads from Inverness, Perth, Stirling and Coupar Angus

there, but has been superseded, and it is possible that the hotel may have been a kingshouse.

Just over a mile beyond White Bridge the realigned military road forks left for Foyers as the B852. Close to the church on the right, and before coming to the present Foyers hotel, was the site of the 'General's Hutt'. There is now a new bridge at Inverfarigaig, but the old bridge can be seen down below. Thereafter the road hugs the lochside, giving evidence of the blasting which was required in the Black Rock area, although recent widenings have tended to make the original building feat look less spectacular. At Dores it joins the A862, entering Inverness by the riverside. From Fort Augustus to Inverness by this route is a drive of scenic beauty, but possibly it is best to reverse the direction and come south from Inverness. Even though most traffic follows the trunk road on the other side of Loch Ness, the military road can be rather busy in summer. In spring or autumn it is much more pleasant.

The original Wade road was more inland. From the point north of White Bridge where the B852 and the A862 fork, it seems to have run roughly parallel to the modern road by Lochgarthside, keeping to the west of Gorthleck and Errogie. The track leading off from Aultna-goire on the Errogie to Inverfarigaig road, going to Oldtown and Torness, and crossing the Farigaig at that point, may be the line. On the other hand, it could strike farther west, crossing the Farigaig just north of Dirichurachan, and thence by the right bank of the Farigaig to join the A862 at 28/26/577279. It certainly skirted Loch Ceo Glais on the line of the A862, after which, according to Roy's evidence, it seems to have forked right at 28/26/598315 on the line of the present minor road, by the side of Loch Ashie, and into Inverness by way of Essich. Having been abandoned after only a few years, this road is very difficult to trace with any accuracy in the Foyers area.

Dunkeld to Inverness

Between Dunkeld and Inverness the military road and the present main road part company in a number of places, and some of these divergences provide interesting walks of varying lengths. The road from Edinburgh and the south terminated at the inn at Inver, opposite Dunkeld, on the right bank of the Tay. Inver, of course, will always be associated with the meeting of Robert Burns and the equally famous Scottish fiddler, Niel Gow. Until the building of Telford's bridge over the Tay, there was a ferry from Inver to the opposite bank. On both banks the remains of the former jetties are visible, 49/52/015425 and 49/52/015424. Tradition has it that, in misty weather, a cow used to swim ahead of the boat to show the ferryman the way! On the Dunkeld side of the river, junction is made with the road coming past the cathedral from Coupar Angus. From then onwards there is a well-defined road, which has been maintained as an estate road, past Dunkeld House Hotel. Thereafter the road runs pleasantly beside the river for about two and a half miles before joining the modern road at Ledpettie (Map 5). Bridges and culverts have been modernised, but two bridges, one at 49/52/005440 and the other at 49/52/005456, show definite signs of older military construction. From Ledpettie the line is approximately that of the present road, probably going straight on through Dowally instead of bearing left, and then through Kindallachan instead of bearing right.

About a mile beyond Ballinluig, at 49/52/977538, up to the right, can be seen part of the old road and a bridge, known as Prince Charlie's Bridge. Rudimentary traces of the road can be followed in the wood for about half a mile, after which it crosses the present road to Moulinearn, now a farm, but formerly an inn, or kingshouse, the first on the road north after Inver. It was at this inn that Sir Alexander Mackenzie, the pioneer in Canada, died in 1820. Just beyond the former inn are the remains of a military-type bridge. From Moulinearn the minor road going up to the right, and running for almost a mile above the main road, may have been the original line, but there is no clear evidence on this point. Thereafter the line appears to be that of the present road until the outskirts of Pitlochry, where the military road, instead of going under the railway bridge, went straight on by what is now the access road to Dundarroch Hotel, after which it is lost amid modern road and rail works. It reappears for a short distance just above the Troopers' Den, beyond the National Trust Information Centre at Killiecrankie, as a grassy track leading past the hotel, before ending ingloriously in a rubbish dump beside the village hall.

At a lodge opposite Kingsisland, 48/43/887647, the old road sweeps up to the right, turning left approximately on the 500ft contour, below

Lude House, passing Kilmaveonaig church and making straight for the Old Bridge of Tilt. From that point onwards, the road tends to coincide with roads maintained by Atholl estates. It is, indeed, probable that General Wade made use of existing estate roads, relieving the estate of the necessity for maintenance. From the Old Bridge of Tilt there is a 2½-mile stretch of military road which can be fairly easily followed. From Old Bridge of Tilt follow the existing road to the fork at 48/43/873664. Keep straight on between the wall and the line of trees to St Bride's chapel, and up the side of the yard to the former kingshouse of Old Blair, now the estate factor's house, then across the bridge over the Banvie burn, the lower part of which may be 'military'. The road then skirts Diana's Grove, going straight on through the field gate, the line being clearly traceable between pairs of trees planted at about 200yd intervals, before striking off to the left to come down on to a well-defined portion leading to Woodend, after which parts can be traced to the West Lodge, including part of an old bridge in the garden of the lodge.

Between West Lodge and Pitagowan the road seems to have been on the line followed by the railway, as traces can be seen on either side of the line. The present service road to Baluain and Balnacroft may well have been the line of the original road, crossing the Bruar where the railway bridge now is. From Pitagowan the line is clearly visible, striking diagonally upwards through the moor on the right of the present road to Calvine, where it crosses the Minigaig path to Ruthven. From here is a very pleasant 2½-mile walk. Passing through Clunes wood the road crosses the Allt a Chrombaidh by a spectacular military-type bridge, the Drochaid na h-Uinneige (the eye of the window), thrown across the torrent. Just above Clunes Lodge the road is lost for about 100yd in a steading, but is easily picked up again on the other side. Shortly after this it crosses a burn by a pretty, but rather decayed military bridge; this bridge and approaches are an excellent example of what the old road must have looked like. This part of the road joins the present main road at 48/42/773683. The green line of it is clearly visible to anyone coming south on the A9 (Map 6). There are broken remains on either side of the modern road, including a longer stretch on the right, just before Dalnamine Lodge, with a double arch of the post-military period, which was in use during the writer's youth. About a mile from Dalnamine, on the left, is the junction of the military road from Stirling and Crieff, just before Dalnacardoch, a former kings-house and now a shooting lodge. This was a major road junction and the situation was of some importance.

On the right-hand side of the road, opposite Dalnacardoch, at the end of the last cottage, the military road can be seen climbing the hill before descending to Edendon Bridge, a toll house on the nine-teenth-century road. The modern bridge supersedes an older bridge, and immediately on the other side the military road strikes off again to the right on a very visible grassy track. Thereafter it follows the line of electric pylons, across the remains of a bridge over an unnamed burn at 48/42/712709, rejoining the present road at a quarry 48/42/702715. From Dalnacardoch to this point is quite a pleasant walk within visual distance of the present road.

After about half a mile on the A9, there appears on the right an un-mistakable landmark, the Wade Stone, with a short stretch of the military road, ending in a ruined bridge over the Allt an Stalcair. The Wade Stone is one of the major marking stones on the north road. The general, who was a tall man, is reputed to have put a golden guinea on top of the stone one year, and to have reached up the following year to recover his coin! Marking stones were, of course, essential on High-land roads, just as marking posts are at the present day.

After another half mile, at 48/42/679717, to the north of the present road, there is a further 200yd stretch, with a ruined bridge over a burn. The military road then climbs up to follow the line of pylons, crossing two bridges, one of them ruined, before rejoining the present road at 48/42/661725. As it comes down to the A9, there are the remains of a bridge at 48/42/659725. After yet another bridge, some 200yd beyond, the road climbs once more to the line of the pylons until, just south of Dalnaspidal, it is almost a quarter of a mile from the present road, cross-ing the Allt Coire Mhic Sith by the now ruined Oxbridge, the site of the original ox-feast. It remains on this level for about another mile before gradually coming down once more. From then onwards it is more or less coincident or contiguous with the present road until it reaches the restored military bridge on the left, just about a mile from Dalwhinnie. At this point it crossed the Truim, but any signs beyond have been completely obliterated by the railway. There may have been another bridge leading into the Ericht Hotel, a former kings-house, or the river may just have been forded.

About a mile farther on, just past the distillery, at 37/42/641857, the military road can be seen going straight on instead of bearing left, carrying on through a rubbish tip, and back across the railway to join the A9 about half a mile on. It was from here that the Corrieyairack road to Fort Augustus branched off. From this point, the line is virtually that of the present road until just south of Crubenmore Lodge, where at 37/42/672900 the military road can be seen striking off through the grass to the left, going behind the lodge and swinging round to cross the Truim, just south of Crubenmore school, by a picturesque little bridge at 37/35/676914. On the west side of this bridge it is joined by the link road from Ruthven to Catlodge on the Corrieyairack road. From the bridge the road can be faintly traced crossing a field, the railway, the modern road, and the field on the right, before joining the road by Etteridge to Phoines. The double-arch bridge on the right, just north of Crubenmore Lodge, is part of the early-nineteenth-century realignment (Map 7).

From Etteridge the military road runs past Phoines, almost dead straight, by Milehouse of Nuide, for a distance of about six miles, to within a mile of Ruthven Barracks. It is drivable as far as Phoines, thereafter it is a walking road, pleasant with good views, meeting the present B970 at 37/35/753990. Ruthven Barracks was, of course, a major staging post of considerable strategic importance. Reputed to have been originally a stronghold of the Wolf of Badenoch, the hill, possibly partly man-made, on which the castle originally stood, was an obvious place for the building of a barracks in 1719. Had General Wade been allowed to make the Glen Feshie road, which would have terminated at Ruthven, the strategic position of the barracks would certainly have been as important as that of Fort Augustus.

The road from Ruthven crossed the flats to the Spey, where there was a ferry at Boat of Kingussie, opposite the kirk, where it continued up Boat Road (now Manse Road) to meet the A9. After a short distance on the line of the present road, it turned north by the farm track to Kerrow, turned right just to the south of Kerrow and Laggan, behind Lynchat, to Balavil, the house built by James Macpherson, of Ossian fame (Map 8). From here for the next two and a half miles is a very

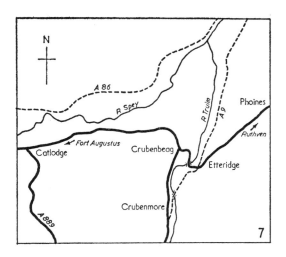

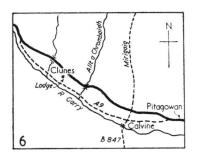

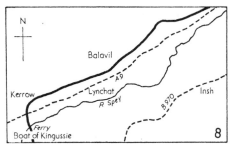

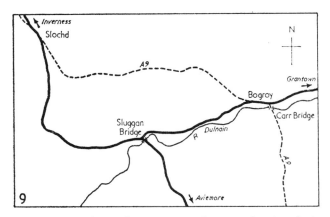

6 The Calvine area; 7 The Crubenmore-Etteridge area, showing the junction of the roads from Ruthven, Dalwhinnie, and the Corrieyairack; 8 The Kingussie area; 9 The Carr Bridge–Slochd area, where the Grantown road meets the Dunkeld to Inverness road at Sluggan Bridge

pleasant walk, parallel to the modern road, and gradually coming down to meet it, past a ruined chapel, at 37/35/824048. A few yards downstream from the present bridge over the Allt na Baranachd are signs of a former bridge. From this point the road goes through a birch wood on the right of the A9 to the Suie Hotel at Kincraig. It may, thereafter, have followed the present railway line for about half a mile. A fine stretch, through a wood of old Scots pines, with a wonderful view of the Cairngorms, can be found by turning right at the gate of Alvie Lodge, then turning left after about 200yd at 37/35/844068. The road is lost just beyond the railway bridge at 37/35/860084, but according to the cartographic evidence of both Roy and Taylor and Skinner, it seems to have followed the line of the railway to Alvie, where it went off to the right along an existing track, turning left after about 200yd, and running very close to the river before once more coinciding with the railway, emerging at the entrance to Aviemore as a track beside a garage. There was a kingshouse at Aviemore, and a junction road from Grantown on Spey, through Boat of Garten, joined the Inverness road at this point.

There are traces of the military road almost all the way, on the left, from Easter Aviemore to Kinveachy. From the lodge gates at Kinveachy there is a fine seven-mile stretch of military road, with fine views back to the Cairngorms, as it climbs the Kinveachy side of the hill before dropping down to Sluggan Bridge across the Dulnain river. Though not the original bridge, it is old and picturesque, and though damaged, it is usable by walkers. The Duthil road to Grantown and Fort George comes in just on the north side of Sluggan Bridge. This clearly visible road strikes off to the right, coming up to the A9 at Bogroy, just north of Carr Bridge. From Sluggan, the Inverness road is well defined as it skirts northwards round Inverlaidnan hill to join the present road at Slochd (Map 9).

Just over the brow of Slochd Mòr the military road strikes off to the right, giving another pleasant three-mile walk to Raigbeg, where it comes down to the Findhorn by a steep hill at the side of the school. The river is now crossed by a modern bridge, at the north end of which the military road goes straight ahead up the hill and through the wood to join the A9 on the sharp left-hand bend just beyond the railway bridge at Tomatin 28/27/803292. From the Tomatin end the grassy outline is very clearly visible in the field. About a quarter of a mile farther on another well-defined part of the road can be seen going straight on for nearly a mile from the drive entrance to Tomatin House 28/27/798296, behind Freeburn Hotel, alongside the river, with traces of a bridge at 28/27/797300. It comes up to cross the A9 at the milestone 28/27/794317, crossing the railway, then looping down to rejoin the A9 at Dalmagarry, where there was a kingshouse (Map 10). From there to the school at Moy, traces are visible on both sides of the present road. Opposite the school at 28/27/775337 it strikes off to the left to give a good five-mile walk, though soft in places, to the river Nairn, which is crossed by the Faillie Bridge, a pleasant old bridge, but not the original (Map 11). Once across Faillie Bridge the road runs straight into Inverness, a distance of about $5\frac{1}{2}$ miles, and is known as the Old Edinburgh Road.

The military road from Dunkeld to Inverness provides several walks varying from a few hundred yards to seven miles, although it will be seen from the map that the seven-mile walk from Kinveachy to Slochd Mòr can easily be broken into two almost equal parts. None of these walks present any real difficulty provided that waterproof footgear is worn. It should be remembered that in wet weather the military roads can be something of a general wade!

(The current realignment of the A9 trunk road will alter considerably the topography of the military road, which in some sectors will actually be overbuilt.)

Stirling to Dalnacardoch

It is pointless to try to find any remains of the military road between Stirling and Dunblane, but the long straight after the Victoria School is obviously the original line. At Greenloaning it forks left as the A822 for Crieff, going through Braco and passing the Roman Camp at Ardoch. Then at 54/58/846118 the military road, instead of turning right as the main road, goes straight on along what is now a pleasant minor road, running almost ruler-straight to Muthill, apart from a double bend at Lurg. At Muthill it rejoins the A822 and goes dead straight until it reaches the bridge over the Earn at Crieff. Thence it goes on up the hill, across the A85 Perth to Lochearnhead road, and up

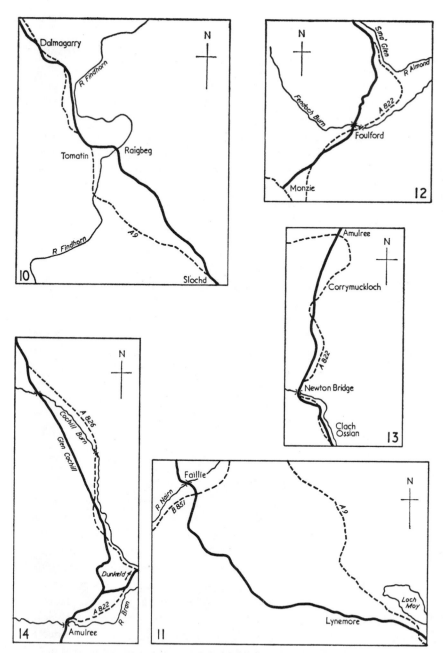

10 Slochd to Dalmagarry; 11 Moy to Faillie Bridge; 12 The Sma' Glen area; 13 The Newton Bridge area; 14 The Glen Cochill area, the junction of the Dunkeld road with the Stirling to Dalnacardoch road

to the now-demolished mansion house of Ferntower, on the side of the Knock. So far, on this route, there have been several of the long, straight stretches which are typical of the military roads at their best. It is impossible to determine the exact line of the road over the side of the Knock, but it can be picked up again at the entrance to Monzie Castle, 55/52/884242, running up between two dykes to join the A822 at 55/52/884244. It then follows the straight part of the modern road to 55/52/885249, where it can be seen starting up among the trees to the right. There is a substantial wall on the uphill side of the road, and the stumps of a former line of trees. There are the remains of a bridge at 55/52/891260 over the burn, beside the ruins of a former settlement. Thereafter the line of the road is very faint, ending in a field about 200yd short of Foulford Inn. So far it has been a pleasant, but not outstanding walk.

Just past Foulford Inn, at 55/52/898268, the military road goes off to the left into the Sma' Glen. This is a very pleasant walk of rather less than two miles, rejoining the modern road at 55/52/904295. There is a small triple-arch bridge at 55/52/899269, and at 55/52/901274 a well-repaired single-arch bridge over the Fendoch burn. The road then climbs by a hairpin bend and through a ford before crossing another bridge. It is difficult to tell whether subsequent burns were originally crossed by fords or bridges, but some buttressing can be seen before the road comes down to the A822 (Map 12). There follows a short spell on the modern tarmac before the military road diverges slightly to the right, passing Clach Ossian, after which it crosses the present road, cutting off the corner, and coming down to the cottage at 48/52/893312. A short distance beyond Newton Bridge the road veers off to the left, crossing the Lurg burn by an old bridge, going alongside Meall Reamhar for about a mile and a half. This part is rather wet for walking. It returns to the modern road at 48/52/892337, crosses to the right for a short spell, then at 48/52/892343 it cuts off to the left, going up behind Corrymuckloch farm, before coming down to the road junction at Amulree (Map 13). Apart from one fence, this, again, is quite a pleasant walk. Amulree Hotel was originally a kingshouse (there is a fine example of a cheese press in the garden), and after crossing the Bran at 48/52/902368, the road goes on as a well-defined track, by the side of Ballinlochan farm, to a ruined bridge across the

Fender burn. The track then becomes rather overgrown and rough and has been encroached on by a forestry plantation for about 200yd. After this, it comes down to the present road at 48/52/912395, crossing to the right for about half a mile, then recrossing to the left at 48/52/908405. For the next three and a half miles through Glen Cochill, the going tends to be wet and unpleasant, with the alternative of taking to the rather high heather. It is a good walk for active people who do not mind getting their feet wet, and who can do a long jump of about eight feet! The underside of the bridge at 48/52/908405 is old enough to be interesting. The road clings to the lower slopes of Meall Dearg, and here there are many marking stones, some of which show boreholes for gunpowder. Even in April snow drifts can fill the road completely. At the bottom of Glen Cochill it is extremely marshy. From 48/52/892435 to 48/52/888441 the road is built up on a causeway along which a burn now flows, and there are three other bridges in less than a hundred yards. Two are quite sound, but the third, across the Cochill, is in ruins, and here the burn is both deep and swift. After this the road bends sharply right and comes up to the modern road at 48/52/888445 (Map 14).

For the next mile, passing Loch na Craige, the military road winds quite visibly from one side to the other of the present road, before crossing from the milestone on the bend 48/52/879464 to the right. Thence there is a track somewhat obscured by afforestation with marking stones for rather more than half a mile, with a small bridge at Gatehouse. Thereafter it can still be traced, on the right, through a field, and then by a well-marked track through a birch wood. At the bend 48/52/875481 it crosses to the left, though this is not easy to see, going along the higher ground, to come down at 48/52/872484. From here it probably carried straight on to 48/52/869485, though all traces have been oliterated by cultivation, after which, though it is a bad state, it is readily traceable down to the hospital at Aberfeldy. It is possible to walk from Crieff to Aberfeldy, avoiding the modern road for much of the distance.

In Aberfeldy is the Tay Bridge, erected by General Wade with almost loving care, and appropriately, beside it, the monument commemorating the raising of the Black Watch as a regular regiment of foot. The original line was not, unfortunately, through the poplar-lined avenue, but diagonally to the left, rejoining the present road just after the Weem Hotel, which proclaims, correctly, that General Wade stayed there while directing the bridge-building operation (Map 15). From this point onwards the military and modern roads are largely coincident. The hotel at Coshieville is reputed to have housed troops during the making of the road, and it is claimed that the walls were originally loopholed.

There are small and not easily seen traces of the old road between Glengoulandie and White Bridge, where there was once an inn. This bridge has been rebuilt at a different angle from the original. Another short stretch can be seen on the left not long after passing the Foss road. On the left, just before crossing the graceful Tummel Bridge, was a kingshouse, now converted to a dwelling-house.

From Tummel Bridge the military road goes left towards Rannoch before turning right, by Bohespic, and, having climbed to the top, it runs almost dead straight for nearly two miles. Not only is it a wonderful stretch of road, but it also affords magnificent views. Indeed, from the scenic point of view it is probably better to come from the opposite direction. About half a mile downhill on the left, beside the Allt na Moine Buidhe and near the farm of Moulin a Mhadaidh, so-called because it was at the old meal mill here that the last wolf in Rannoch was killed, are what local legend calls 'General Wade's Barracks' (Fig. 2). The foundations, rudimentary walls and gables are still standing, cheek by jowl with nineteenth-century sheep buchts. The buildings were single storied, probably thatched, as there is no trace of roof material among the tumbled stone. It has, however, now been established that they are a relic of the government's 1763 scheme to settle demobilised service men in townships on the land. The landowners were justifiably sceptical, and most of the soldiery, lacking agrarian skills, were, on the whole, uninterested and uncooperative. In 1781 the Blackpark settlers, who among other things, refused to do their statute labour, were given notice to quit. (see, *The Jacobite Estates of the Forty Five*, by Smith, A.M., p.145 seq.)

The road then drops down to Trinafour, cutting off from the modern road, through a bank of rhododendrons to the church and the old bridge. There was also a kingshouse at Trinafour. From the bridge

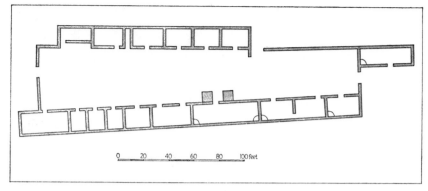

Fig 2 'The Barracks' at Blackpark near Moulin a Mhadaidh (48/52/715609).

the road climbs up by a series of well-engineered traverses, the final one being a very tight, but easily negotiable hairpin. From the top the views are magnificent. At 48/42/727683, just beyond a little bridge, the military road can be clearly seen going down to the right through the heather. At the bottom nothing remains of the bridge over the Allt Culaobh except the piers, but there is usually so little water that the crossing is easy. The modern road is rejoined at 48/42/725690. Before coming to the bridge across the railway, there is a short length of road on the left, making straight for Garry Bridge over the railway. This is another of Wade's bridges, still in use and well preserved. Unfortunately, since hydro-electric operations, there is now little water in the Garry except in times of spate. The road then joins the Dunkeld to Inverness road just short of Dalnacardoch (Map 16). Both from the point of view of walking and enjoying wonderful scenery, the road from Crieff to Dalnacardoch ranks high among the military roads.

Dalwhinnie to Fort Augustus

The most famous of all the cross roads is the route from the central Highlands to Fort Augustus over the Corrieyairack pass. From the south the approach is from Dalwhinnie, by the A889, to Catlodge.

138

From the north the present access is by the A86 from Newtonmore, but in earlier times it was from Ruthven Barracks, by Etteridge, across the railway, turning down the little road to the right, crossing the old bridge, past Crubenmore school, up along the forestry road to join the minor road at spot height 972, and so by Breakachy to Catlodge. From Catlodge, where the two roads meet, the route is westwards along the A889/A82 to the farm road junction at 37/35/605936. There is a fine old military bridge across the Mashie Burn at 37/35/600936, then rather a rough track past Dalcholly House, by the Spey, to the junction at 37/35/583935, joining the tarmac minor road from Laggan (Map 17). From this point to beyond Shirramore much of the old road has been obliterated by waterworks, and there is a bridge over a now dry burn at 37/35/555932. At Garbhamòr is the former kingshouse, now, alas, in a state of growing disrepair, which is a great pity, because in such a position it is ideally situated to serve as a hostel for those wanting to cross the Corrieyairack (Map 18). Whether or not it was a barracks rather than a kingshouse is of minor importance. It was used by all, soldier and civilian, who had to cross the pass. It is unfortunate that the box bed was, some years ago, removed and sent to the museum in Fort William, where it was labelled 'General Wade's Bed'. Just beyond the kingshouse is the fine Garbha Bridge over the Spey, surely one of the best of the Wade bridges. From here the actual ascent of the Corrieyairack starts. There are typically long straight stretches of military road, and a car can safely be taken as far as Melgarve. For those whose time or walking ability is limited, the distance from Melgarve to Fort Augustus is about twelve miles.

At this point let it be said that the Corrieyairack walk is not difficult. The road rises steadily all the way from Melgarve, climbing about 1,000ft in two and a half miles, leaving only about 500ft to climb from the start of the hairpins to the top of the pass. These hairpins or traverses were well buttressed, and when kept in repair, must have been a remarkable sight. They are now rough but quite easy to walk. There is, too, an abundance of wild life in an area like this. The writer has seen blackcock at the foot of the pass and a wild cat on the eighth traverse. From the top of the pass, and on the way down, there is an appealing wildness of scenery. There is a military bridge still over the Allt Coire Uchdachan, and a short distance farther on, a bailey bridge,

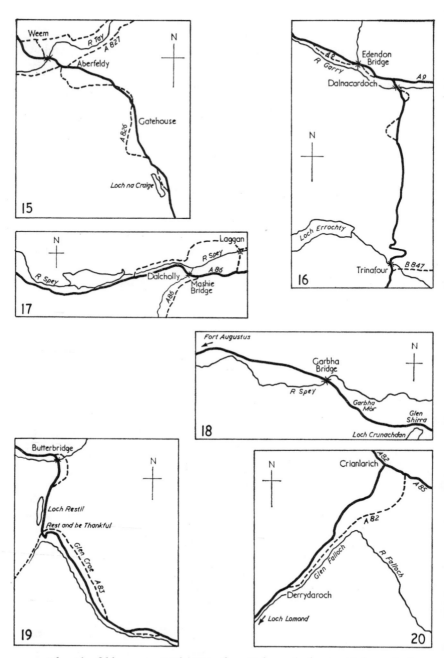

15 The Aberfeldy area; 16 The Trinafour–Dalnacardoch area: Dalnacardoch is the meeting-place of the roads from Stirling and Perth to Inverness; 17 Approach to the Corrieyairack (1); 18 Approach to the Corrieyairack (2); 19 Rest and Be Thankful area; 20 Glen Falloch area

built in 1961, over the Allt Lagan a' Bhainne, by 278 Field Squadron of the Royal Engineers. On this side the road drops 1,500ft in five miles, undulating quite gently before traversing more steeply as it approaches Cullachy. It joins the Fort William to Inverness road just over a mile from Fort Augustus. Spectacular and beautiful as other military roads are, they all must yield pride of place to the Corrieyairack.

Argyllshire Roads

Dumbarton to Inveraray

There are a few but scarcely significant traces of the old military road between Dumbarton and Tarbet. There is, for example, an old bridge near Inverbeg, but successive realignments and works of reconstruction have obliterated most of the original road. Of course, it should be remembered that in the case of most lochside roads, there is little scope for realignment. The work has, of necessity, to be done on the existing line, and usually means widening, supporting or buttressing and levelling off the inclines. Half-way between Tarbet and Arrochar, at 53/56/304043, part of the old road, very wet and overgrown, can be traced for about half a mile into Arrochar. Thereafter, small bits are visible on either side of the A83, including about half a mile on the right, between 53/56/259043 and 253043, in Glen Croe. Then from 53/56/248046 up to Rest and Be Thankful, is the well-defined old road down below, to the left of the present road, which was reconstructed in the 1930s. The old road itself was a reconstruction of the original military road. As it climbs up to Rest and Be Thankful, there are good examples of later buttressing and traversing and, of course, at the top is the commemorative stone, just by the car park. For walkers this is a two-mile stretch, easy to walk underfoot, but leaving no one in any doubt as to why the top of the hill is called 'Rest and Be Thankful'! The view from the top compensates for the effort expended.

Just about a mile further on, at 53/56/234087, there is another stretch, cutting the modern wide corner, and crossing the Kinglass Water by a fine old bridge at Butterbridge, just before rejoining the A83 (Map 19). The old road then runs alongside the present road all the way to Strone, where it becomes the access road to and from Cairndow, by the side of Loch Fyne. The Cairndow by-pass was made in 1932. From Cairndow to Inveraray there are stretches of the old road contiguous with the new, with a fine old bridge over the river Fyne, and another over the Gearr Abhainn. From Loch Lomondside the route is one of considerable scenic beauty, but only on the short stretches indicated is it worth-while to go on foot. There is far too much traffic in summer to make it either safe or worth-while to walk on the present main road.

Crianlarich to Tarbet

From the walker's point of view the connecting road from Crianlarich through Glen Falloch to Tarbet gets off to a good start. The approach is just opposite the railway bridge at 53/50/379256. Indeed, the first of the little bridges can be seen from the A85 just as it leaves Crianlarich. It climbs up the hillside above Keilator and keeps above the present road for three miles, coming down just above Derrydaroch, where it is obliterated by a railway bridge over the Eas Eonan (Map 20). Just below the railway bridge are two piers of a bridge built at the time of the first realignment, but now superseded by the present road. From this point onwards there are periodic traces of the old road, but on Loch Lomondside modern roadworks and the railway have destroyed most of the original road. At Tarbet the old road goes up behind the hotel to join the Arrochar road. Whether the traveller turns off here for Inveraray, or goes straight on to the end of Loch Lomond, the route is one of considerable beauty, but heavily overloaded with traffic.

Inveraray to Bonawe and Tyndrum

Roy's map shows quite clearly the road north from Inveraray going up the left bank of the Aray for about three miles before crossing the right bank. This was an estate road which may originally have been used by the military authorities. The wooden bridge across the river at this point 53/50/089130 is at present unusable, and is obviously far from having any claims to antiquity. Taylor and Skinner's road maps of 1776 show the road on the right bank of the Aray all the way, so that obviously the original line was abandoned at some time between 1757 and 1776. There are numerous examples of this first military realign-

142

ment completely grassed over, and of the second realignment, still with some tarmac on the surface, both north and south of this point.

Just about half a mile north of the wooden bridge, there is a part of the old road, beside the river, from 53/50/089135 to 53/50/085140, with a typical little bridge over the burn. There are faint and very boggy stretches from 53/50/093184, where the modern road bends right at Taynafead, by the monument, to 53/50/099207. The line can be seen quite clearly from the A819, over on the left, but unless there has been a lot of dry weather, it is not recommended. From this spot for the next few miles, there are fine views of Cruachan which completely dominates the scene.

Until the late 1930s the road went through Cladich, but since then the present by-pass has been made. About two miles from Cladich road-end, and just beyond Achlian, the original road goes off to the right, making straight for Dalmally, by way of the monument, a prominent landmark. This was the main road until the 1930s, and is still drivable, with care, but it is a road which is a 'must' for the walker. To get the best from it, it should be done from the Dalmally side. The view of Cruachan and Loch Awe from the top must be one of the finest in Scotland. It is an easy three miles, and should present no walking difficulties to anyone.

From Dalmally the road branches left for Bonawe and Taynuilt, and right for Tyndrum. The old road to Bonawe, however, did not skirt the lochside as at present. It turns left at the Dalmally Hotel, and after going up by the side of the church and manse, crosses the Orchy by a fine three-span bridge. Thereafter, it becomes the B8077, going by way of Stronmilchan, and crossing the river Strae by an old bridge, where there may have been an earlier ford, and coming down to the A85 just about a mile from the Loch Awe Hotel. From this point there are traces of the original road farther up on the right, but modern road works, hydro-electric activity, and the railway have obscured most of it (Map 21). Once through the Pass of Brander, the old road turns sharply right at the Bridge of Awe, and goes under the railway and on to the power station. To this point it is a pleasant tarmac road with passing places, but from then onwards it degenerates into quarries and stone working. From Dalmally to the power station it is a good road with fine views.

The road from Dalmally to Tyndrum carries on straight past the hotel. At 53/50/196275 the old road through Glen Orchy can be seen quite clearly going off to the left, and there is an old stone bridge at the other side of the road. Just beyond the entrance to Strone farm, on the left, is the start of a two-mile stretch of the old road through Glen Lochy at 53/50/207275. At first it is not very visible, and is very wet, but it soon becomes clearly seen up on the hillside, coming down at 53/50/235276. From this point there are many little loops to left and right where the modern road has been straightened. Then at 47/50/264306 there is another well-defined two miles up to the left, with sundry bridges. From here, 47/50/296317, to Clifton, where it joins the Stirling to Fort William road, there is nothing of significance. There are about four miles of walking on the old road in Glen Lochy. It is easy but not spectacular. These two parts were the main road until the 1930s.

Stirling to Fort William

From Stirling the road went by Doune and Keltie Bridge to Callander and the Pass of Leny, where a short length of the old road can be seen. Then, just before St Bride's Chapel, the old road goes off to the right, round the wooded hillock, past Anie, and comes down to the A84, across a ruined bridge, just opposite the car park at the end of Loch Lubnaig. The total length is rather less than a mile, and it can be very wet underfoot. It is obvious that the line up the lochside must have been the same as it is now. Just across from Laggan farm and south of Strathyre village is a regimental stone, with the date 1769, and other letters which seem to indicate that the regiment concerned was the 4th Regiment (the King's Own Royal Regiment). By 1769, of course, the work was obviously repair and maintenance. Beyond Strathyre is the Kingshouse Hotel, an inn of considerably greater antiquity than the eighteenth century, but one of the only two hotels still using the name of Kingshouse.

About half a mile from Kingshouse, at the milestone 54/51/567207, the military road, partly obliterated by drainage trenches, can be seen going off to the left. It can be traced through the birch wood, on the edge of which is a small ruinous bridge. It then goes through the wood,

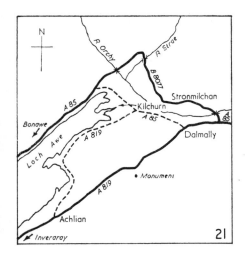

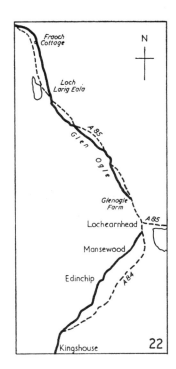

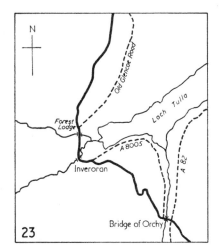

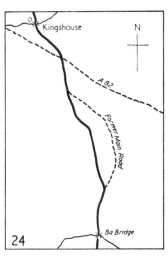

21 Dalmally–Loch Awe area: junction of the roads from Tyndrum, Inveraray and Bonawe; 22 Glenogle area; 23 Black Mount area (1): the original military road, the former main road and the present main road (A82); 24 Black Mount area (2)

crossing the former railway line, crossing the Kendrum burn on a wooden bridge, under which old stone piers are visible, past Edinchip House to Mansewood where, at the railway bridge at 54/51/584229, all traces disappear. There is little doubt that it was destroyed when the long-abandoned Crieff to Balquhidder railway was made, and that it followed that line behind Lochearnhead Hotel to the entrance to Glen Ogle.

The next clear trace of the road can be picked up at Glenogle farm, from which, to the bridge by the modern roadside at 54/51/579256, there is a pleasant, grassy half-mile. For about 350yd it coincides with the present road, after which it can be seen down to the left in the valley, where there are also three bridges. It comes up and crosses the A85 just by the railway bridge before Loch Larig Eala, marked by the double wooden pylons. It then goes up to the right, round the shoulder of Beinn Leabhain, marked by the metal pylons. Near Glenoglehead Crossing it descends to the level of the wooden pylons as far as the transformer station near Fraoch cottage (Map 22). At 54/51/552297 the military road goes off to the left, joining the service road to Wester Lix about 200yd from the house, and crossing the burn by a small bridge. It then passes north of the outbuildings, crosses the former railway, goes through the plantation, and comes down to join the modern road at Ardchyle farm. There are several traces to the left of the present road between Ardchyle and the former Luib station. From this point to Crianlarich, the line may well have been that of the railway. At Crianlarich the start of the road through Glen Falloch to Loch Lomond can be seen quite clearly at 53/50/379256. From here to Tyndrum there are a few insignificant stretches to be seen, but from Tyndrum to Fort William, a distance of about forty-eight miles, there is no need for the walker to use the modern road at all.

From Tyndrum to Bridge of Orchy the military and the old Glencoe roads are virtually coincident. The bridges, though old, are mostly very much later than the military building period. The road turns up right by the shop at Clifton, and from the top of the hill runs beside the railway, on the opposite side of the valley from the new road, through Auch, and along the lower slopes of Ben Dorain, before crossing the A82 to Bridge of Orchy. As soon as it crosses the bridge, it makes straight for Inveroran over Mam Carraigh, with a traverse in the middle. The Bridge of Orchy end has been somewhat obscured by forestry planting.

At Forest Lodge, beyond Inveroran, the walker is well advised to keep to the Old Glencoe Road on the lower level, rather than try to find the line of military road higher up, as it is extremely boggy, and almost invisible at the Forest Lodge end (Map 23). The two roads meet just before Lochan Mhic Pheadair Ruaidh, cross Bà Bridge together, and separate once more at 47/50/280498, before joining once more just short of Black Rock cottage. Again, it is probably better to keep to the lower road. Shortly after Black Rock cottage the military road crosses the present road to arrive at the other Kingshouse which is still a hotel (Map 24). The walk from Bridge of Orchy to Kingshouse is about eleven miles, is not difficult from either direction, provided that the advice given above is followed, and from the scenic point of view can hardly be bettered. On a clear day, far across Rannoch Moor, Schiehallion can be seen.

From Kingshouse the military road runs along the lower slopes of Beinn a' Chrulaiste, marked by the pylons, before coming on to the present road near Altnafeadh, the start of the Devil's Staircase. At this end the Staircase is a track rather than a road nowadays. It goes off to the right between the house and the burn before climbing up in a series of easy hairpins. It can be rather rough and wet, but presents little difficulty, and gives the walker wonderful views of Buachaille Etive Mòr. From the top there are equally spectacular views of the Mamores to the north. The road descends to cross the Allt a' Choire Odhair-bhig by a ford. Winding rather more than is apparent on the map, it crosses the Allt a' Choire Odhair-mhoir by a scaffold bridge, a replacement of an older bridge. This is rather a wet part, and one of the features is the number of paved cross drains, which were a feature of the military roads before culverts were made. From the pumphouse on the pipeline at 47/41/201604 the military road goes off to the left. It has been made up by British Aluminium, and descends by a series of easy traverses to the lochan at the foot of the Allt Coire Mhorair, before running into Kinlochleven. This walk is under six miles, and if transport can be arranged at either end, it can be done easily and is richly rewarding.

The continuation of the road to Fort William is equally spectacular.

Opposite the school in Kinlochleven there is a notice, 'Public Footpath to Fort William by the Lairig Mhor'. To go all the way involves a walk of about eleven miles, but it can be reduced to about six miles by arranging to be met by car at Blar a' Chaoruinn (Map 25). The initial climb is quite rough and steep, but from the top there is a fine view of Loch Leven and the Glencoe mountains. The first part of the road at the top has been made up and well maintained, with good bridges of varying ages. About half a mile from Tigh na-sleubhaich the original road can be seen up to the right for about half a mile, now a wet and grassy track. From here, past Lairig Mòr cottage, the road is much rougher, with numerous paved cross drains and fords, but presenting no real difficulties. A track from Callert, on Loch Leven, can be seen quite clearly coming down to Lairig Mòr cottage. This was an unofficial summer route, often used by the soldiers after the Devil's Staircase had been abandoned, and the road had been made through Glencoe. From Blar a' Chaoruinn to Fort William there is a single-track tarmac road, with some fine views of Ben Nevis on the right, and of the entrance to the Great Glen straight ahead. With a little planning, the whole distance from Tyndrum to Fort William can be covered in easy stages, and if the weather is good, the walker can enjoy some of the finest scenery in Scotland.

In 1785 the Devil's Staircase and Lairig Mòr were abandoned in favour of a road through Glencoe to Invercoe, later to become the Old Glencoe Road, crossing Loch Leven by ferry to Callert, then following the line of the present A82 by Onich to Fort William. A road bridge now carries the A82 over Loch Leven from south to north Ballachulish.

Coupar Angus to Fort George

As far as may be ascertained, the road from Coupar Angus to Blairgowrie was on the line of the present road, and the long straight into Blairgowrie looks typically military. From Blairgowrie to Bridge of Cally, however, the military road followed a completely different line from that of the present road, and it makes a very pleasant walk, apart from some seasonal difficulties near the Blairgowrie end. Starting from Lornty Bridge the road zigzags up, past the farm on the right. From then onwards to the top of the hill, the road becomes a very rough track, and unless the undergrowth has been cut, rather difficult. Once at the top of the hill, however, the going becomes easier. Though cultivation has caused the line to disappear at 49/53/164487, the track is good thereafter, passing west of Easter Mause, Hilltown of Mause and Middle Mause. Just before Dykeside it bends left before going dead straight across Cochrage Moor for nearly two miles. In parts the heather is quite high, but the line is clear and distinct, and must be regarded as one of the best remaining stretches of military road for walkers. There is a ruined bridge near Dykeside with the date 1875. At the highest point, 49/53/151503, there is a circle with banks the same height as those bordering the road. Its purpose is completely unknown. There are another two such circles, one on each side of Dalnacardoch. It seems unlikely that they were passing-places, otherwise there would have been many more. Nor can they have been sentry posts or, again, there would have been more. It may well be that they were of later date, and were connected with the shooting activities carried on in both areas. The road went through the thicket in the wood at 49/53/147506, before descending to Bridge of Cally by a series of zigzags and a well-defined track.

After coming round to the front of the hotel at Bridge of Cally, the road then goes through a gate at the side of the building, upstream for a distance of about seventy yards, where it crossed the Ardle by the original bridge, of which the vestiges of a pier remain. It then came back on the opposite bank, through the garden of the post office, and up by what is now a flight of steps to the houses at the top of the hill, coming out at 49/53/142516. Thereafter it climbs the hill on the left, opposite the road to Rannagulzion, continuing until it rejoins the main road at 49/53/137531. At South Persey Farm the modern road bears right, but the military road went straight on, crossing a bridge over the burn, and ending in a field, where cultivation has obscured its subsequent course. Although there is little or no trace, it seems obvious that it went straight through to the former inn of Persey at 49/53/140551 (Map 26). From this point onwards there is nothing to be seen until Lair, where the road went straight on between 49/43/142636 and 49/43/143637. Thus far the only part to be recommended to the walker is the stretch from Lornty Bridge to Bridge of Cally which, apart from the hazard already mentioned, is easy and pleasant.

The bridge at Spittal of Glenshee is a military-type bridge with strengthening. At 41/43/132751 the military road goes off to the right, about half a mile from the shepherd's cottage. It passes through a sheep bucht, beyond which there is a single arch of a bridge, before coming up to the present road about half a mile farther on. It follows the former main road until just before the Devil's Elbow, after which it goes along the bottom of the valley and up to what is now a car park at the summit of the pass. (The Devil's Elbow has now been straightened and debris has encroached on the military road.) It follows the main road to the ski lift, beyond which a half-mile stretch can be seen up to the left. From this point it crosses the A93, following the Cairnwell Burn to the bridge at its junction with the Allt a' Garbh Coire, continuing on the right side of the burn for about half a mile before rejoining the present road. From then onwards traces are visible, particularly at the Glen Clunie AA Box, on both sides of the A93, until reaching Fraser's Bridge, the double-arch bridge on the left, which takes the military road off on a different line altogether, coming into Braemar by the side of the golf course. Traces of the original road can be seen normally to the left of the present line of this road. For a full treatment of this part of the road from the Spittal to Braemar the reader is referred to an article by Mr Angus Graham on page 212 of volume 97 of the *Proceedings of the Society of Antiquaries of Scotland* (1963–4).

From this point the road passed in front of Braemar Castle, which was, of course, one of the government forts, before crossing the Dee by the old Invercauld Bridge, a wonderful specimen of eighteenth-century bridge building. Thereafter there is doubt, endorsed by G. M. Fraser in *The Old Deeside Road* (1921; p 220), as to whether the military road went northwards by Felagie and Abergarder or followed the present line to Inver. Certainly at Inver there are traces of what could have been the pre-military road to the left. Flanking the present road are the two granite pillars which held the toll bar in later times. Other traces are visible before the military road turns up at 41/37/252953, over what is now a fairly rough track to Bush Lawsie. From this point the line is the same as that of the modern road, to a point about four miles beyond the fine Gairnshiel Bridge. At this point, 42/37/297064, the present road veers right, but the old road goes straight on, coming

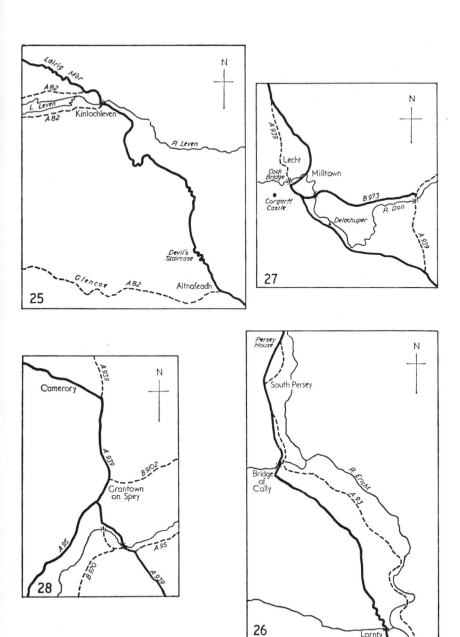

25 Devil's Staircase–Lairig Mòr area; 26 Blairgowrie–Bridge of Cally area;
27 Corgarff area: junction of the roads from Aberdeen and Coupar Angus to
Fort George; 28 Grantown area: junction of the roads from Coupar Angus
and Aviemore to Fort George

down to the right bank of the Don, passing the Youth Hostel at Delachuper, before rejoining the A939 about half a mile from Corgarff Barracks. This is a pleasant walk of just under three miles, passing several ruined bridges, and presenting no difficulties. Corgarff was a castle of some antiquity which, according to the minister of the parish in the *Old Statistical Account*, had been 'purchased by government in 1746 from Mr Forbes of Skellatur, and for several years thereafter, 15 or 20 men were stationed in it; for some years past [1794] the garrison has consisted of 2 or 3 invalids' (volume 13, p 182). For a fuller treatment of the castle the reader is referred to an article by the late Dr Simpson in volume 61 of the *Proceedings of the Society of Antiquaries of Scotland*, page 48.

It is clear from cartographic evidence of maps in both the National Library of Scotland (Z/3/35 b) and the British Museum (XLVIII, 68), that from the castle the road crossed the Cock Burn, then the Don, before climbing the Lecht, not by the present line, but by Milltown, to the right of Allargue House, joining the present road at 41/37/253117 (Map 27). The present route is by way of Cock Bridge, which takes its name from the inn, the sign of which used to be a red cock. Nearly four miles on, at the Well of the Lecht, on the right, is the well-known stone recording the date of construction and the regiment responsible. On the outskirts of Tomintoul, at Alltachbeg, the military road went straight on instead of forking right like the present road, and at the milestone at the other end of the town, the old road went straight on instead of branching left, rejoining the A939 at Urlarmore, just before Bridge of Avon. About half a mile farther on, just after the road to Fodderletter, the military road, instead of taking the modern loop to the right, went straight to 38/36/133209. For about four and a half miles after Bridge of Brown, the present road follows the military line, then on the bend, just after Lynebreck, the military road once more went straight on for about half a mile, crossing a much overgrown bridge. It joins the A95 just before crossing the former railway line outside Grantown on Spey, crosses the Spey on the old military bridge, and rejoins the main road at 38/36/034269.

Leaving Grantown, the A939 to Dava is probably the military road. Shortly after crossing under the former railway line, it branches left at 38/36/033308, going through Camerory and past Anaboard to rejoin the present road at 29/27/009352, a pleasantly walkable stretch (Map 28). At Dava, just after the school, the military road is the A939, turning sharply left. After about a mile and a half it went straight between the two Aitnochs, instead of by the modern right loop, on its way through Refouble to Dulsie Bridge, thrown like a spectacular challenge across the Findhorn. From Dulsie Bridge the road takes the shortest route to Fort George, turning sharp left at Clunas for Glengeoullie, and going sharp left again to cross the Riereach burn. At Inchyettle it forks left instead of entering Cawdor, and after an elbow bend at Dallaschyle, it crosses the Nairn. From Clephanton it goes in an almost dead straight line to Ardersier and then to Fort George.

For those who prefer driving to walking, this road, almost all the way, varies from the pleasant to the spectacular, and where a car cannot be taken, except by way of modern diversions, the walks are well worth doing. It is also a road from which other routes may be explored. From Crathie the Deeside road may be followed to Aberdeen, or branching off at Banchory, the military road may be followed back over Cairn o' Mount. From Corgarff the Donside road leads back to Aberdeen. From Grantown or Dulsie Bridge, military roads may be followed to Aviemore, and from Fort George a military road leads to Inverness. For those who are interested, this road forms a wonderful axis for exploration.

Coupar Angus to Dunkeld and Amulree

There are some divergences between the military road and the modern road. The old road breaks off from the A923 about a mile and a half north of Isla Bridge at 49/53/195427, skirting Stormont Loch, and going in a dead straight line to a point on the A93 opposite Upper Gothens farm. The track is rough, but drivable or walkable. From the A93 to Upper Gothens the line has been obscured by cultivation, but it can be followed as a farm track to the road junction at Chapel of Lethendy. Thereafter it follows the B947, by Kirkton of Lethendy to the A984 (Map 29). Where the present road bends left at 49/53/119413, the old road can be seen going straight on towards Spittalfield. Beyond Caputh, at 49/53/065405, where the present road bends left, the military road went straight on, along what is now the drive in to Dungarthill.

It degenerates into a rough track going off to the left in the wood at 49/53/062406, coming down to the A984 on the bend just opposite Newtyle farm. It branches off to the right once more as a narrow, single-track tarmac road at 49/53/037422, coming straight down the hill, crossing the main street of Dunkeld, through the square and past the cathedral, before carrying on either to join the start of the Inverness road or crossing the ferry to Inver. The inn at Inver was much frequented, because on it converged travellers from Edinburgh and Stirling to cross the ferry before the days of Telford's bridge. It was here at the end of the eighteenth century that Niel Gow used to play for the guests.

From Inver the military road and the B898 coincide for about half a mile, after which the former branches left along what is now the road leading to the Hermitage where, in times of spate, the falls are magnificent. From here the road goes through Craig Bhinean forest along what is now a well-defined forest track, debouching on the little road up from Rumbling Bridge, and continuing up the hill above the left bank of the Bran, crossing the Ballinloan burn by a good, military-type, single-arch bridge. It then takes a long, strange, hairpin-like sweep to climb the hill before coming down past Drumour to join the A822 at Aldville. It continues along the A822, ignoring the junction with the A826, then turns sharp right at 48/52/917377 to join the Crieff to Aberfeldy military road about a mile from Amulree, at 48/52/909377.

Fort Augustus to Bernera

To get on to the Fort Augustus to Bernera road it is necessary to leave Fort Augustus on the A82 for Inverness, follow the sign to Jenkins Park, then take the second turn on the left, past the church, to the forestry houses. Beyond the gate and quarry the first zigzags can be seen going up to the right. Although there has been modern maintenance on this road, the traverses and bulwarks are worthy of note. In particular the walker will be amazed at the ease of the climb. The road continues through the gate with the sign 'Inchnacardoch forest', goes up through the trees and crosses under the electric cables. From the top there is a wonderful view of the Great Glen, Fort Augustus, the line of

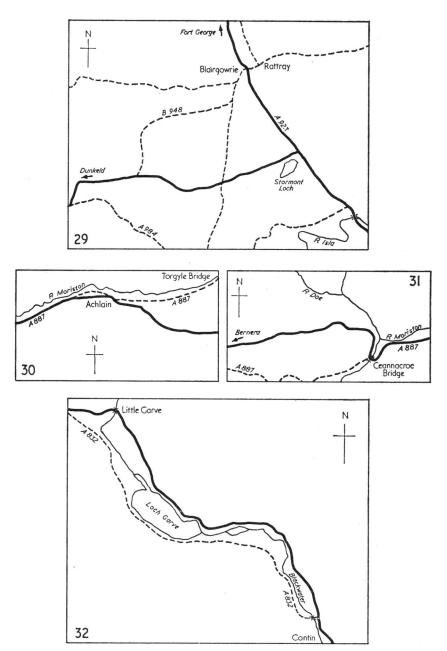

29 Blairgowrie area: junction of the road from Dunkeld with the Coupar Angus to Fort George road; 30 Ceannacroc area (1); 31 Ceannacroc area (2); 32 Contin–Garve area

the Caledonian Canal, and right across to the Corrieyairack. It is worth going to the top just for this. If the walker continues, there is a very pleasant walk of just over six miles, coming down through Ceannacroc Forest to meet the A887 at Achlain. At this point the modern road bends to the right, but the old road can be traced going straight on, cutting the corner (Map 30). There are also traces in the field on the right, from 36/34/275116 to Spot Height 395. It then crossed the river where Ceannacroc Bridge is, probably taking a line through the Coille Ghormaig. Samuel Johnson claimed that the inn at Aonach was nine miles from Fort Augustus, which must have placed it quite near to Ceannacroc Bridge, but there is now no trace of it.

Just north of Ceannacroc Lodge the line can be picked up with some difficulty, after which the military road runs as a track for about four and a half miles, gradually coming down to the present road at the side of Loch Cluanie, at 36/34/156104 (Map 31). There is another stretch of about one and a half miles coming up from Lundie cottage, and going up the hill to the right, before coming down to the present road at 35/33/111111. From this point until it reappears, just round the corner from Cluanie inn, the line of the old road probably lies under the loch. From 35/33/073115 the military road goes up to the right above the A87 for another mile and a half, coming down again through the wood at 35/33/039117. Between this point and the bridge at the battle site, traces of the old road, on the right, have been virtually destroyed by recent road widening. It is possible that the military road went off to the left at 35/33/971139, coming down again at 35/33/963147. Thereafter the line seems to be that of the present road to Shiel Bridge.

From Shiel Bridge the road climbs the hairpins of Mam Ratagan, from the top of which is a view which must be one of the finest in Scotland—the Five Sisters of Kintail, Beinn Fhada and Loch Duich all merging into a wonderful panoramic composition. From the descending road to the left is Beinn Sgritheall on Loch Hourn, with Skye straight ahead. At the end of the road are the ruined barracks of Bernera and the short Glenelg ferry to Skye. A few miles from Glenelg village, up Glen Beag, are two fine Pictish brochs, Dun Telve and Dun Trodden. Skye, itself uniquely spectacular, could scarcely be approached by a more spectacular route.

Contin to Poolewe

It seems probable that the military road left the line of the present road about half a mile north of Contin, on a well-defined track through the forest, keeping to the left bank of the Black Water, passing the Falls of Rogie, and crossing the railway to reach Loch Garve. It virtually disappears in the Coill 'an Achaidh Mhoir, but emerges again as a service road on each side of Strathgarve Lodge. It crosses the Black Water by the beautiful military-type bridge at Little Garve, and thereafter its line must have been approximately that of the A832 (Map 32). The water levels of lochs have, of course, changed since the eighteenth century, and the railway may also have destroyed traces, but the original road, military or not, probably followed the south side of Loch Achanalt. There are remains of earlier road works between Loch a'Chroisg and Kinlochewe, but to make any claims on their behalf would lack the backing of the necessary evidence.

The Northern Link Roads

Sluggan Bridge to Dulnain Bridge

This road can be seen clearly as a track going up through the wood at the northern end of Sluggan Bridge. It emerges on the A9 two miles later at Bogroy, just north of Carr Bridge, and can be quite a pleasant walk. From Carr Bridge the road is the A938 to Dulnain Bridge.

Grantown to Aviemore

The road leaves Grantown as the A95, crosses Dulnain Bridge, and branches south, following the line by Skye of Curr to where it joins the present main road at 38/36/972225, after which it makes its way straight to Boat of Garten. From here it goes slightly west of the former railway line, running beside it on a well-defined track for over a mile and a half before striking over towards Aviemore, reaching the main Inverness railway line at 37/36/905147, after which it presumably followed the line of the railway the short remaining distance to Aviemore. It is quite a pleasant walk as far as the railway.

Dulsie Bridge to Aviemore

This is the present B9007, coming down past Lochindorb to Duthel on the A938. It provides a drive through typical moor and peat bog.

Grantown to Forres

The line is the same as that of the Coupar Angus to Fort George road as far as Dava Bridge, where it strikes off, crossing the Divie, then following the Findhorn to Forres as the A940.

Fort George to Inverness

The road leaves Fort George as the B9006 and forks right at Ardersier as the B9039. It joins the A96 at Newton before running into Inverness past Allanfearn.

The Military Roads in the North-East

Fettercairn to Fochabers

At Fettercairn this road starts as the B974. It climbs steeply up the Cairn o' Mount, where the summit is almost 1,500ft above sea level, and from which there is a wonderful panoramic view. It drops more gently on the northern side, and just over a mile and a half from the rather pleasant Bridge of Dye, it divides. The right fork, remaining on the right bank of the Water of Feugh, eventually crosses the Bridge of Feugh to join the Deeside road at Banchory.

The left fork crosses the Water of Feugh by Whitestone Bridge, before crossing the Dee by Telford's Potarch Bridge. It then follows the A93 to Kincardone O' Neil, where it forks right at 39/37/589997, as a minor road to Lumphanan. It leaves Lumphanan as a minor road, reaching the junction of the A980 and the A944, crossing the Don by the Bridge of Alford and, continuing as a minor road to Clatt, it reaches the A979 by way of Kirkhill of Kennethmont. It follows the A979 to 30/29/526314, where it went on by what is now the railway track to Gartly Station, to bend sharply left on to the A97 for Huntly. It leaves Huntly as the A96 for Keith, carrying on as the same road to Fochabers.

Stonehaven to Fochabers and Portsoy

The road leaves Stonehaven as the A92 for Aberdeen. It leaves Aberdeen as the A96, by Tyrebagger Hill and Kintore to Inverurie. It continues as the A96 through the Glen of Foudland to Huntly. It continues, of course, as this road to Fochabers, the Portsoy branch being the B9022.

Corgarff to Aberdeen

After fording the Don near Corgarff, and again at Colnabaichan, this road keeps south of the river. There are few traces in the early stages, but it runs as an unclassified road by Heughhead, Rippachie and Towie, eventually reaching the A944 at Whiteley. There is some doubt as to whether it forked left as the B993 by Monymusk and Kirktown of Kemnay before joining the A96 about half a mile south of Kintore, or whether it went to Aberdeen as the A944, past the Loch of Skene. Both roads were in use at the time.

The Deeside Road

The genuinely military part of this road has already been described as part of the road from Coupar Angus to Fort George. From Crathie to Banchory there are many stretches of old road to be seen, but for the reasons discussed before, the road is much more likely to be civilian than military.

The Dumfries and Galloway Road

From the evidence available, the military road from the Water of Sark started on what is now the A6071, turning along the present B721 at Springfield, through Gretna Green, then joining the B721 just west of Gretna, and remaining on this line until it crosses the Annan. It then swings south to follow the B724 by Cummertrees, Clarencefield and Mouswald, rejoining the A75 at Collin, and so on to Dumfries, via Annan Road, zigzagging from Loganbarns to Eastfield Road and Hoods Loaning, where traces cease.

The road left Dumfries by Howgate Street and Laurieknowe on the approximate line the A711 by Cargen Bridge, leaving it at the west end of Cargen Bridge to follow what is now the unclassified road by Lochfoot to Haugh of Urr, joining the A745 just outside Castle Douglas. On the west side of Castle Douglas the military road leaves by Carlingwark Street, crossing the B736 at the Buchan end, by way of Threave House and Rhonehouse to the old Bridge of Dee. Immediately across the bridge it turns sharp left along the village street, on to Greenhall, and across a field to join the A75. From here through Ringford to Twynholm the route line was approximately that of the A75. The military road comes in at the back of Twynholm Village Hall and goes down to the bridge, continuing along the south side, before turning right just before the cross-roads at the school. Thereafter it goes by Barluka, crossing the A75 just north of Enrick.

To Gatehouse the line is that of the A75, thence by Ann Street and High Street, crossing the Fleet Bridge and turning right, up the Station Road to Blackloch, before bending back to Anwoth Kirk. From Roy's map it is interesting to note that the pre-military road made for Anwoth Kirk in an almost straight line from the bridge. It is still marked, in part, at least, by a somewhat rudimentary path. From Anwoth Kirk to Glen there is a good and pleasant three-mile walk, including a typical hairpin bend. This is a walking part of the road (Map 33). Cars should go by the road from Skyreburn Bay to Glen. The road over Corse of Slakes is a very pleasant walk or drive, with fine views of typical Galloway countryside. The pre-military road went off left from Lauchentyre and Glen much higher up the hill before coming down again at Glenguicken Moor. Near Burns there has been some realignment, the present road bearing right where the military road went straight on along the high bank of the Balloch burn to Hills (Map 34).

From Creetown the military road left by Barholm Bridge, crossing

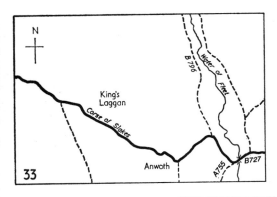

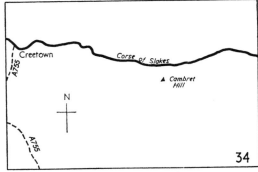

33 Corse of Slakes area (1); 34 Corse of Slakes area (2)

east of the road through Creetown, where, as in the case of some Highland roads, the line has been obscured by the former railway. It joins the present minor road at Graddock Bridge up to the Old Palnure Bridge at 80/83/458644, thence by the old Lead Mines and Path Brae to Blackcraig. Just beyond the A712 it runs straight behind the Minnigaff council houses, then turns left along Macgregor Drive to rejoin the B7079. It then goes through the grounds of Cree Bridge Hotel, in line with the old Cree Bridge which is about ninety yards upstream from the present bridge.

Once across the bridge the road followed the line of the A714 through Newton Stewart, turning right, up Princes Street, at 80/83/411652, past the cemetery, then on the line of the former railway to Black Park, where it veers right by Moor Head before coming down to the A75 at 80/83/353633. It crossed the Bladnoch by the Shennanton Bridge, turning sharp right, then coinciding with the line of the pylons by Ardachie and Kildarroch to a point about half a mile beyond Halfway House, where it peters out. From Black Park to this point there is a walk of about six miles, including half a mile on the main road.

It is possible that from here to just beyond Barlae the line was the same as that of the A75. It can be picked up again at 79/82/265600, crossing and recrossing the former railway for about four miles, and coming into Glenluce at the Glenjorrie service road. Again this is quite a pleasant walk.

The military road appears to have had the same line as the A747 and the A75 from Glenluce to Castle Kennedy, where it forked left at 79/82/109597, meeting the A75 again at 79/82/077607. It left Patrick by the 'Old Port Patrick Road', by way of Crailloch, Knockglass and Enoch to the A77.

As far as the Stranraer to Ballantrae road is concerned, there has been so much reconstruction work between Stranraer and Cairnryan that it is doubtful if any traces of the old road remain. Beyond Cairnryan, the old road may have gone farther up the hill towards Little Laight, after which there is no trace for just over a mile. Although it is difficult to be definite, the military road is probably the little road branching off left from the A77 at 79/82/052724, crossing the Water of App, passing Craiganlea House, crossing the Water of App again by a pleasant bridge, and going up by the side of Glenapp Kirk, after which it disappears in a cultivated field. From here to Ballantrae the line was probably that of the present road.

Abbreviations used in Notes and Bibliography

Albemarle	Albemarle Papers
Boswell	*Journal of a Tour to the Hebrides*, by James Boswell
Burt	*Letters from a Gentleman in the North of Scotland*, by Edmund Burt
GD	SRO Documents
HRB	Reports of Commissioners for Highland Roads and Bridges
Hist Papers	Historical Papers Relating to the Jacobite Period
JHC	Journal of the House of Commons
Johnson	*Journey to the Western Islands*, by Samuel Johnson
KWB	King's Warrant Book
Knox	*A Tour through the Highlands of Scotland*, by John Knox
MCS	Minutes of the Commissioners of Supply
MS	National Library Manuscript
Maitland	*Commissioners of Supply for the Stewartry*, by Charles Maitland
NBB	North Britain Book
NSA	*New Statistical Account*
OSA	*Old Statistical Account*
PRO	Public Record Office
Pennant	*Tour in Scotland*, by Thomas Pennant
Pococke	*Tours in Scotland 1747–60*, by Bishop Pococke (SHS edn)
RSGS	Royal Scottish Geographical Society
SHS	Scottish History Society
SRO	Scottish Record Office
Southey	*Journal of a Tour in Scotland*, by Robert Southey
TBP	Treasury Board Papers
TGDAS	Transactions of the Dumfries & Galloway Antiquarian Society
TGSI	Transactions of the Gaelic Society of Inverness
TISS	Transactions of the Inverness Scientific Society
TMB	Treasury Minute Books
WO	War Office Records

Wordsworth *Journal of a Tour in Scotland*, by Dorothy Wordsworth

NB   Numbers in italic type denote a volume in a series; following
          numbers indicate a page or folio

Notes

Introduction

1 MCS Inverness, *1*, 83v, 84r
2 MS307, 197
3 MS308, 217
4 JHC, *37*, 580; *39*, 509
5 29 Geo III, c 42
6 Cunningham, A., *The Loyal Clans*, 168
7 Albemarle, *2*, xxxviii
8 For fictional treatment see Munro, N., *The New Road* (1919)

Chapter 1
The Wade Era, 1724–1740

1 Burt, *2*, 254–64, 268–84
2 Hist Papers, *1*, 147–9
3 MS7187, 45. General Wade recorded in 1725 that 'Edmund Burt under the Privy Seal of Scotland' had been appointed 'Receiver General and Collector of the unsold Forfeited Estates in North Britain'. This establishes that Burt's christian name was Edmund, not Edward, and makes clear the type of work he was doing in the Highlands
4 Burt, *2*, 293–309
5 MS7187, 86r & v; MS308, 239; MS309, 38
6 Hist Papers, *1*, 150–65
7 MS7187, 83v; Hist Papers, *1*, 151
8 JHC, *20*, 718; *21*, 38. See also Appendix B
9 MS7187, 97v
10 JHC, *20*, 714; *21*, 40; *20*, 4
11 KWB, *31*, 413–14
12 JHC, *21*, 38; *23*, 391; MacWilliam, 10; Wade Letter in Fort William Museum
13 Wade Letter in Inverness Museum

Chapter 2
The Caulfeild Era, 1740–1767

1 MS7187, 118r
2 MCS Perthshire, *1*, 50r
3 Albemarle, *2*, 503
4 JHC, *25*, 29, 70, 202, 239, 245, 246, 272, 444, 445, 515, 679, 779
5 Albemarle, *2*, xxxii–iii; xxxiv–end of introduction; *1*, 202
6 Ibid, *1*, 138, 210, 227
7 25 Geo II, c 41
8 Ferguson, *Scotland from 1689 to the Present*, 152
9 WO 26:21, 262–3; MS304, 74r
10 WO 26:21, 356–66; Hist Papers *2*, 513–84 for detailed reports
11 MS304, 102r; 105r & v
12 MS306, 8v; see also Chapter 3
13 MS307, 217; MS304, 140v
14 WO 26:21, 363; MS308, 190–1; Skelton, *Military Survey of Scotland,* RSGS 1967
15 WO 26:21, 364
16 MCS Perthshire, *2*, 68r

Chapter 3
The Gentle Art of Road Making

1 Burt, *2*, 189
2 MS307, 194
3 Skelton, op cit, 4
4 MS308, 183–98 *passim*
5 TGDAS, *28*, 120–34
6 MS308, 180; MS305, 206r
7 MS7187, 76
8 HRB, *1*, 9–10
9 MCS Perthshire, *1*, 43r
10 HRB, *4, 43 Report*, 3
11 NBB, *10*, 348; *11*, 120, 268–9; TBP, cclxxxiv, No 2
12 MS308, 82
13 MS304, 145r & v
14 MS305, 208r; MS308, 105; MS307, 196
15 MS306, 15
16 MS305, 208, 213; TGDAS, *28*, 120–34
17 MS7187, 115v; Plate 5; MS308, 183; MS305, 208; Chapter 6
18 MS304, 132
19 MS307, 177–81

20 Ibid, 225–6
21 Ibid, 234, 270–2
22 WO 26:21, 404
23 TMB, 27, 192; KWB, 24, 19

Chapter 4
The Wade Roads

1 MS7187, 84–8, 92v
2 Hist Papers, 1, 162; MS7187, 98v, 102v
3 KWB, 30, 380; 31, 4–6; Burt, 2, 214
4 MS7187, 117v, 115r, 116v; also KWB, 30, 5
5 KWB, 31, 219; 32, 273–4
6 Pennant, 216; Pococke, 99
7 Johnson, 25–6, 27
8 WO 1, 615, 593; JHC, 33, 321, 639; 35, 116; 36, 75; 37, 196; 38, 376
9 HRB, 1, *Papers Relating*, 24, 58
10 HRB, 4, *1 Report*, 29; 2, *9 Report*, 4
11 Hist Papers, 1, 162; also MS7187, 98v
12 MS7187, 102r & v
13 KWB, 29, 448–9, 308
14 Culloden Papers, 1, 109–11
15 KWB, 29, 448–9; Culloden Papers, 3, 41
16 WO 1, 615, 593; Pennant, 119; see also Appendix A
17 JHC, 32, 654; 33, 321, 639; 34, 125, 559; 35, 116, 624; 36, 75, 722; 37, 196, 722; 38, 376, 941; 39, 509. HRB, 1, *Papers Relating*, No 1, 23
18 HRB, 1, *Telford's Report*, 5
19 Grant, E., *Memoirs of a Highland Lady* (1911 edn), 40, 166
20 HRB, 1, *3 Report*, 43–4; *6 Report*, 12
21 HRB, 1, *Papers Relating*, 53, 55, 56, 58
22 Grant, op cit, 166–8, 277–8, 298
23 HRB, 2, *8 Report*, 42; *5 Report*, 7; *9 Report*, 18; 1 Geo IV, c 47
24 HRB, 3, *14 Report*, 43; *9 Report*, 4
25 Information supplied by Scottish Development Department
26 KWB, 29, 484
27 SRO GD/1/53/97
28 KWB, 30, 117–19, 218–20; 31, 4–6; 32, 86; MS7187, 117v; More Culloden Papers, 3, 100
29 MS306, 1v
30 JHC, 34, 559
31 HRB, 1, *Papers Relating*, 23, 56; 3, 27
32 TBP, 105, No 7; KWB, 34, 154
33 MCS Perthshire, 1, 35r

34 KWB, *34*, 527, 576–8
35 MCS Perthshire, *1*, 66v, 68r, 97r
36 KWB, *30*, 188, 327–9
37 Wade Letter in Fort William Museum
38 Chambers, *3*, 562
39 Burt, *2*, 204
40 KWB, *30*, 328–9
41 WO 1, 615, 593; JHC, *34*, 559; *35*, 116; *38*, 376
42 HRB, *2*, *8 Report*, 42, 4; *4*, *14 Report*, 5
43 KWB, *31*, 217–20, 413–14
44 NBB, *2*, 245–6

Chapter 5
The Caulfeild Roads

1 TGSI, *38*, Argyllshire Roads, 335, 336
2 TBP, 114, No 26; KWB, *35*, 490; JHC, *24*, 746
3 TGSI, *38*, 350
4 Pococke, 262
5 Burt, *2*, 352
6 MS306, 1v; JHC, *25*, 245
7 MS306, 1v
8 MS307, 57, 73
9 MS306, 1v, 2r, 6r & v, 7r, 8v; MS307, 249
10 Pococke, 62–5
11 TGSI, *38*, 350
12 WO 26:21, 364; MS307, 194; TGSI, *38*, 350
13 MS307, 235, 247
14 WO 26:21, 404
15 TGSI, *38*, 350
16 WO 1, 615, 593
17 Pennant, 241; Pococke, 62–5
18 JHC, *32*, 654; *33*, 321, 639; *34*, 125, 559; *35*, 116, 624; *36*, 75, 722; *37*, 196, 722; *38*, 376, 941; *39*, 509
19 HRB, *1*, *Papers Relating*, 23; *2*, *8 Report*, 42, 49
20 Southey, 247, 249, 251
21 Minute Book of the . . . Trustees and Subscribers to the Road from Crianlarich to . . . Glenfalloch, fols 1–8
22 MS308, 185, 194, 199, 221, 282
23 MS309, 205, 272
24 MS306, 11r
25 KWB, *41*, 203
26 Pococke, 63

27 WO 1, 615, 593; also references as for Note 18 above
28 Minute Book . . . Glenfalloch
29 TGSI, *22, Bighouse Papers*, letter 24
30 WO 26:21, 364
31 TGSI, *38*, 352
32 KWB, *41*, 203
33 Pococke, 63
34 WO 1, 615, 583 (*Ligonier's Order Book*)
35 Pennant, 237
36 TGSI, *38*, 352
37 MS309, 205, 272; MS306, 11r
38 TGSI, *38*, 354
39 Johnson, 143–4; refs as for Note 18 above
40 Refs as for Note 18 above
41 MCS Stirlingshire, vol 1757–85, 30 April 1773
42 MS306, 8v
43 WO 26:21, 404, 364–5
44 British Museum Maps, K xlviii, 66b, Caulfeild Report
45 Ibid
46 PRO Map WO 78/1905, No 4009, & 78/1905/2, No MR479
47 MS308, 183
48 Ibid, 183
49 Ibid, 186
50 Ibid
51 Ibid, 189
52 Ibid, 190
53 Ibid, 184
54 Ibid, 277
55 Ibid, 280
56 Ibid, 282
57 Ibid, 297
58 Ibid, 319
59 MS309, 205, 272
60 MS304, 140v
61 MS306, 15r
62 WO 1, 615, 593
63 JHC, refs as for Note 18 above
64 Pennant, 229–33
65 JHC, *41*, 868; General Mackay's Report to the Treasury, 1785
66 OSA, *8*, 335
67 HRB, *1*, *Papers Relating*, 21–6
68 Ibid, 50
69 Ibid, 11–19
70 Ibid, *2*, *8 Report*, 42

71 Ibid, *3 Report*, 49
72 Ibid, *9 Report*, 15
73 Ibid, 4
74 MCS Perthshire, *1*, 51r, 55v
75 MS306, 8v; TMB, *31*, 16 May 1748
76 WO 26:21, 404; MS307, 177r, 194–5
77 British Museum Maps, K xlviii, 66b & 67
78 MS305, 215v, 216r
79 British Museum Maps, K xlviii, 66b
80 Ibid, No 74; MS309, 205
81 MS306, 11v, 12r
82 MS304, 151v, 156r
83 MS306, 15r
84 Ibid, 18v
85 MS309, 205; Pococke, 104
86 MCS Perthshire, *3*, 37r; *2*, 86r
87 OSA, *19*, 358
88 Refs as for Note 18 above
89 OSA, *17*, 205; HRB, *1*, *Papers Relating*, 28, 55
90 MCS Perthshire, *2*, 1r, 32r
91 Ibid, *3*, 10
92 Ibid, *1*, 27r, 52r, 65r, 64r, 76, 89r
93 Ibid, *1*, 105, 118, 127; *2*, 86, 127; JHC, *34*, 559
94 MS305, 215v, 218r; MCS Perthshire, *2*, 68r
95 JHC, *36*, 75, 722
96 MCS Perthshire, *3*, 129
97 HRB, *1*, *Papers Relating*, 21
98 JHC, *25*, 680; TGSI, *39/40*, Glenelg, 322, 325–6, 327
99 Wordsworth, 91, 107. Dorothy Wordsworth remarked that the barracks at Inversnaid, from which the garrison 'had been withdrawn within the last thirteen or fourteen years', was now 'inhabited by some wretchedly poor families'
100 British Museum Maps, xlviii, No 63, 60b & 62 n.d.; WO 26:21, 364
101 MS306, 15v, 19r; MS305, 207v, 208r, 228v
102 WO 1, 615, 583
103 JHC, *32*, 901; *33*, 321, 639; *34*, 559; Refs as for Note 18 above
104 Johnson, 30, 32; JHC, *32*, 901; *33*, 639; Johnson 60 seq
105 Johnson, 42; Boswell, 251; Johnson, 78–9
106 OSA, *7*, 130; *20*, 311; *16*, 274
107 HRB, *1*, *Telford's Report*, 13; *3 Report*, 49
108 MCS Inverness, *4*, 115r
109 TISS, *5*, 382 Military Roads
110 WO 1, 615, 583
111 MCS Ross, *1*, April 1767; refs as for Note 18 above

112 TISS, 5, 382
113 Knox, 103
114 OSA, 3, 90; 7, 194
115 HRB, 1, Telford's Report, 23; 6 Report, Appendix E
116 Southey, 150, 164
117 HRB, 3, 14 Report, 36, 46
118 NSA, 14, 97, 236
119 HRB, 1, Papers Relating, 50
120 JHC, 37, 528; 39, 509; 40, 57
121 OSA, 4, 313
122 HRB, 1, Papers Relating, 23; 5 Report, 3; 2, 8 Report, 50; 1, Papers Relating, 50
123 Cadet Gunner Campbell's Survey, PRO Maps, MPHH36, 1/220
124 OSA, 8, 314
125 HRB, 1, 5 Report, 36
126 OSA, 8, 555
127 Ibid, 2, 30
128 Grant, J., Records of the County of Banff, 337–9, 380–3
129 MS308, 309, 332; MS309, 246, 313
130 Southey, 82; JHC, 33, 33, 639; 34, 125, 559; 35, 116, 624; 36, 75, 722; 37, 196
131 MS308, 275, 277
132 WO 1, 615, 583
133 Refs as for Note 18 above
134 TISS, 5, 364 seq, Mackay's Report 1784; HRB, 2, 6 Report, 36
135 OSA, 5, 333, 375; 6, 389; 9, 122. There was no bridge until 1814 when Telford built Potarch Bridge; 15, 471
136 HRB, 1, 3 Report, 56, 68
137 Third Spalding Club Miscellany, 1, 233–4
138 MS305, 216v & r, 223v
139 WO 1, 615, 583
140 Refs as for Note 18 above; also Third Spalding Club Miscellany, 2, 249 seq
141 TISS, 5, 364 seq, Mackay's Report
142 Hist Papers, 2, 504
143 MS304, 130r, 138r; MS305, 57v, 223v
144 British Museum Maps, xlviii, No 73

Chapter 6
The Dumfries and Galloway Road

1 SRO, GD10, 544/1, 546
2 MCS Kirkcudbright, 17 May 1746, 26 June 1748, 4 June 1759
3 TGDAS, 28, 120–34

4 MCS Kirkcudbright, 1 May 1753
5 TGDAS, *28*, 120–34, 24 June 1763, 16 July 1764, 29 October 1763, 8 July 1764, 16 July 1764, 7 October 1763, 22 October 1763
6 WO 1, 615, 587
7 TGDAS, *28*, 120–34, 30 May 1764, 8 July 1764
8 TGDAS, *44*, 205–22 & *45*, 212; also Maitland, 73
9 Refs as for Note 18, Chapter 5, above; also *42*, 697
10 JHC, *37*, 578; *38*, 376; *39*, 509; *40*, 57
11 TISS, *5*, 364 seq, General Mackay's Report
12 MCS Wigtownshire, *1*, 16 July 1790, 4 July 1786
13 Maitland, 89, 73–4, 92
14 MCS Wigtownshire, *1*, 30 April 1795
15 HRB, *1*, *Papers Relating*, 25
16 Maitland, 94–6
17 HRB, *1*, *6 Report*, 34, 41
18 Maitland, 95
19 MCS Wigtownshire, *2*, 152

Chapter 7

The Final Phase

1 TMB, *39*, 90, 335
2 Refs as for Note 18, Chapter 5, above
3 HRB, *1*, *Papers Relating*, 4
4 TISS, *5*, 364 seq, Mackay's Report
5 JHC, *42*, 697
6 TISS, *5*, 364 seq; JHC, *42*, 597
7 HRB, *1*, *Papers Relating*, 36, 33, 27, 21–6, 32, 34, 36–7
8 HRB, *1*, 6, 4; Appendix to Telford's Survey, 23; 7
9 50 Geo III, c 43
10 HRB, *1*, *Papers Relating*, 24–7
11 Ibid, *6 Report*, 10
12 54 Geo III, c 104
13 HRB, *2*, 3–4, 52, 48, 50, 55; *3 Report*, 2
14 59 Geo III, c 135
15 1 Geo IV, c 47
16 46 Geo III, c 155
17 4 Geo IV, c 56
18 25 & 26 Vict, c 105
19 HRB, *4*, *Final Report*, 3

Conclusion

1 HRB, *1*, 22

Appendixes

A: Statute labour

In the course of the eighteenth century most counties made arrangements and got permission for the commutation of statute labour on the roads into money payments. The scheme devised by the Commissioners of Supply for Perthshire was as follows.

> Those liable for statutory service were to be summoned at the morning kirk service on Sunday to bring tools and to work for three days before and three days after harvest.
>
> For each day's failure to attend, a fine of Is 6d was to be imposed.
>
> Each working party was to consist of at least twenty men, otherwise the pay of the overseer would be reduced.
>
> Each ploughgate was to provide two single-horse carts or one double-horse cart, with sufficient drivers and one able-bodied man for filling the carts and working on the road. Those liable for this service could, with the consent of the commissioners, pay 2s per day in commutation.
>
> Any other person liable for statute labour on the roads was permitted to compound for 6d per day.
>
> A working day was defined as being of eight hours.

(MCS Perthshire, *iii*, 70-3)

For the Stewartry scheme see MCS Kirkcudbright, 21 May 1759.

B: The Clans – Loyal and Disaffected

General Wade's analysis of the Highlanders for and against the Hanoverian government in 1725 is given below:

'The underwritten clans belong to Superiors well affected to His Majesty.

The Duke of Argyle	4,000
Lord Sutherland and Strathnaver	1,000
Lord Lovat (Frasers)	800

The Grants	800
The Rosses and Munroes	700
Forbes of Cullodin	200
Rose of Kilraick	300
Sir Archibald Campbell of Clunes	200
	8,000

The two clans underwritten for the most part went into the rebellion of 1715, without their Superiors:

The Athol Men	2,000
The Braidalbin Men	1,000
	3,000

The Clans underwritten were in the late Rebellion, and supposed still to be disaffected to His Majesty's Government:

The Islands and Clans of the late Lord Seaforth	3,000
M'Donalds of Slate	1,000
M'Donalds of Glengarry	800
M'Donalds of Moudairt	800
M'Donalds of Keppoch	220
Lochiel Camerons	800
The M'Leods in all	1,000
Duke of Gordon's followers	1,000
Stewarts of Appin	400
Robertsons of Strowan (and Athol)	800
M'Kintoshes and Farquharsons	800
M'Euens in the Isle of Skey	150
The Chisholms of Strathglass	150
The M'Farsons	220
	11,140

Roman Catholics in the Highlands:

The late Earl of Seaforth: but none of his followers except the Lairds of M'Kenzie of Killewn and M'Kenzie of Ardloch (Lewis and Lochbroom).

Chisholm of Strathglass and his Clan – Most of Glengarry's Tribe are Roman Catholics; but he himself is not.

M'Donald of Moudairt and many of his Clan – M'Leod of Barra (M'Niel) and his Tribe. The Duke of Gordon and the most considerable of his followers.

At present the Earl of Sutherland is Lord Lieutenant of the Counties of

Murray, Nairn, Inverness, Ross, Cromarty, Sutherland, Caithness and Orkney.

List of the most considerable Gentlemen who are well-affected to His Majesty's Government, who inhabit and have estates in the Counties under-mentioned:

Murray	Alexander Brody M P
	Alexander Rose of Kilraick
	Laird of Grant, M P
	Sir Harry Innes
	Alexander Duff of Brachan
Nairn	Alexander Ross Junior
	Mr Brody of Brody
	Mr Forbes of Cullodin, M P
Inverness	The Laird of Grant
	The Lord Lovat
	Mr Forbes of Cullodin
Ross	Mr Rose of Kilraick
	Col Monro, M P
	General Ross
	Mr Munro of Culkarn
Cromarty	Mr Rose of Kilraicke
	Sir William Gordon, M P
Sutherland	The Earl of Sutherland
Caithness	The Earl of Caithness
	Alexander Sinclair of Ulbster
Orkney	The Earle of Morton

(*Authentic Narrative of Marshal Wade's Proceedings*, Burt, ii, pp286-9)

C: Highland Companies

The six Highland Companies formed by General Wade in 1725 were:

Lord Lovat's Company commanded by Simon Fraser, Lord Lovat
Sir Duncan Campell of Lochnell's Company
Colonel William Grant of Ballindalloch's Company
John Campbell of Carrick's Company
Colin Campbell of Skipness's Company
George Munro of Culcairn's Company

These companies, with four newly rasied companies, were fomed in October 1739 into the 43rd (Highland) Regiment, now the 42nd, or the Black Watch.

Lovat's, Lochnell's and Grant's had in addition to their commander, two lieutenants, three sergeants, three corporals, two drummers, and sixty privates. The other three were lieutenant's commands, with one ensign, two sergeants, two coporals, one drummer and thirty privates. The first three were increased in 1727 to a hundred, the other three to sixty.

In a directive to the commanding officers General Wade ordered them to 'take care to provide a Plaid [tartan] Cloathing and bonnets in the Highland Dress for the Non-Commission Officers and Soldiers belonging to their Companies, the Plaid of each Company to be as near as they can of the same sort and colour'. (MacWilliam, H. D., *A Black Watch Episode of the Year* 1731, pp 3-5.)

D: A Highland Funeral

When the Highland Companies were assembled at Ruthven in August, 1731, Ensign Grant, of one of the companies, was killed while trying to stop a brawl. Scottish funerals have been noted for the lavish entertainment provided. Ensign Grant's funeral was no exception.

	£	s	d
To his funeral expences 3 firlats[1] oat meall baiked with Seeds and Butter, fire candle[2] and pains[3]	9	00	0
To likewalk[4] and funeralls 4 Stone[5] Cheese at 4 Sh Str (sterling) p. Stone	9	12	0
To 20 hens kill'd for the funeral entertainment	3	00	0
To 7 Duiks	2	6	8
To 2 gees	1	6	8
To 1 wedder[6]	2	00	0
To 12 wild fowls	1	4	0
To a baccon ham	2	00	0
To 4 Salmon fishes	3	00	0
To 2 Tealizies roast beef[7]	1	4	0
To 1 butter for roasting the fowls	4	16	0
To 1 bottle vinegar	0	7	0
To fire for roasting and boyling the meat	2	00	0
To 17 pints and 1 Chappin aquavit att 20d p. pint[8,9]	17	8	0
To 4 pints east India Rumm att 4 Sh Str p. Pint	9	12	0
To 12 dozen bottles Strong ale att 4d p. pint	14	8	0
To 1 pint white wine	1	16	0
To Dealls for the Coffin[10]	3	00	0
To nails for ditto	0	4	0
To 2 dozen bottles Stong Claret wine att 17d Str p. bottle	20	4	0

Notes:
£1 Sterling = £12 Scots

¹ A firlot = approx. 35 lbs
² Fire candle = fir roots, used as torches,
³ Pains = bread
⁴ Likewalk = watch by the dead
⁵ Stone = probably the 22 lb kebbuck
⁶ Wedder = castrated ram
⁷ Tealzie = a large joint of meat
⁸ Chappin = approx. a quart. (a scots pint = 2 imperial quarts)
⁹ Aquavit = spirits, here probably whisky
¹⁰ Dealls = planks or boards

(MacWilliam, H D, *A Black Watch Episode of the Year 1731*, p 14)

E: Deployment of Troops in Scotland in 1746–7

Cumberland's Army at Culloden
15   Battalions of Foot
1st   Royal Scots
Midlothian (St Clairs)
3rd The Buffs, East Kent (Howards)
4th Royal Lancaster (Barrells)
8th Liverpool (Wolfes)
13th Somersetshire (Pulteneys)
14th West Yorkshire (Prices)
20th Lancashire (Blighs)
21st Scots Fusiliers (Campbells)
25th Scottish Borderes (Sempills)
27th Inniskilling Fusiliers (Blakeneys)
34th Border, Carlisle (Cholmondeleys)
36th Worcestershire (Flemings)
37th Hampshire (Munros, Later Dejeans)
48th Northamptonshire (Ligoniers, later Conways and Batereaus)
Hussars 3rd (Blands)
       10th (Cobhams)
       11th (Lord Mark Kers)
Artillery Train under Colonel Belford
Some Argyleshire Militia

Effective Total 8,811 (Infantry 6,411)

Four days after Culloden Skeltons, Handasydes, Houghtons and Mordaunts regiments arrived at Leith and went on to Inverness.

On 24 May Cumberland went to Fort Augustus, which was to be the main base for the ensuing butchery, taking with him Kingstons Horse and eight regiments of foot, Barrells, Wolfes, Skeltons, Sackvilles, Scots Fusiliers, Houghtons, Dejeans and Conways. A week later, Houghtons relieved Guises in Fort William. The Argyleshire Militia were deployed in Appin, and Loudons Independent Companies in Badenoch and the Cameron country.

Somewhat on the Cromwellian pattern Scotland was divided into four districts, each under a Major General. These districts were:

1. Inverness under Major General Blakeney, commanding Houghtons at Fort William, Loudons at Fort Augustus, Blakeneys and Batereaus at Inverness, Mordaunts at Narin and Handasydes at Elgin.

2. Speymouth to Dundee, under Major General Skelton, commanding Dejeans at Cullen and Flammings at Aberdeen.

3. Perth, under Major General Huske, commanding the Royal Scots, Sackvilles, Skeltons and the Artillery Train.

4. Stirling, under Major General Bland, commanding Barrells, Prices, and Conways at Stirling, the Scots Fusiliers at Glasgow and Lees at Cannongait.

Wolfes, Sempills and Pulteneys were sent to Flanders, Howards Buffs to Carlisle, Cholmondeleys to Newcastle and Kingtons to England to disband.

The army in Scotland remained at that strength until March, 1747, when the Earl of Albermarle, whom Cumberland had left in command, went to Flanders, taking five of the Foot Regiments with him. Two more went in August, 1747, when General Bland took over the command from Albemarle.

The strength state of the army in Scotland on 1 September, 1746, was:

15 Battalions of Foot with an effective strength of	10,324
Loudons Regiment with an effective strength of	2,016
5 Regiments of Dragoons	1,713

With the inclusion of the Artillery Train there must have been at that time over fifteen thousand troops in Scotland, most of them in the Highlands.

The detailed deployment within what was probably regarded as the danger zone was:

Loudons Regiment, based on Fort Aufustus, with Detachments at:

Letterfinlay	1 Subaltern	30 Men
General's Hut (Foyers)	1 Subaltern	30 Men
Garbhamòr	1 Subaltern	20 Men
Dalwhinnie	1 Sergeant	12 Men
Dalnacardoch	1 Subaltern	20 Men
Aviemore	1 Subaltern	30 Men
Blair (Atholl)	1 Subaltern	30 Men (also 1 Captain)

Detachments from other regiments were sent to Coupar Angus, Crieff, Doune, Dunblane, Kippen, Buchlyvie, Balfron and Drymen.

There was also established a 'Chain' from Loch Shiel, by Strontian, Glencoe, Braes of Argyle, Perth, Stirling and Dunbartonshire to the Water of Leven, for 'Distressing Rebels and Securing the Well Affected Subjects in the Above Countries,' No,1 Post at Strontian with detachments at Inversanda and Polloch covered Ardnamurchan and Morvern. No.2 Post at Achtriachtan, with its detachments covered Glencoe, Appin and Benderloch. No.3 Post at Deribeag covered Dalmally, the Braes of Argyleshire and part of Perthshire. No.4 Post at Killin covered Glen Lyon, Crianlarich and Balquhidder. No.5 Post at Drymen covered Glen Falloch, Loch Lomondside and the 'whole of Dumbartonshire'. It was considered that 'this forms a Compleat Line from Strontian to Dunbarton and will effectually prevent any rebels from coming within it.'

Despite the magnitude of the operation, the prize eluded the grasp of the Hanoverian government. Prince Charles Edward escaped to France, and as Albermarle explained to Newcastle 'our detachments have always been betrayed by People that the rebels had on the top of the High Hills, who by some signal agreed on could always convey any intelligence from one to another in a short space of time.'

Even when General Bland assumed command in August, 1747, there were still between seven and eight thousand troops in Scotland, deployed as follows:

Skeltons at Fort William
Handasyde's and the Artillery Train in Perth
Mordaunts – half in Edingurgh and half in Linlithgow/Bo'ness
Blakeneys divided between Montrose, Arbroath, Dundee and St Andrews
Barrells at Stirling
Houghtons in Glasgow
Price's in Inverness
Batereaus divided between Elgin, Banff, Peterhead and Aberdeen
Royal Scots – one company in Cupar and one in Kirkaldy
Lord Johns Murray's Highlanders – three companies between Tarland
        and Taybridge (Aberfeldy)
Loudons – ten companies between Ruthven and Dingwall
St Georges Dragoons divided between Leith, Haddington, Duns and Kelso
Naizons Dragoons divided between Newliston, Ayr, Stranraer and
        Dumfries.

(This note is based on the *Albermarle Papers*, i, pp 201-25; ii, intro., pp xxxii-xlix)

F: Edmund Burt on Road Making

'First, the stony moors... having for surface a mixture of stones and heath. The stones are fixed in the earth, being very large and unequal, and generally are as deep in the ground as they appear above it; and where there are any spaces between the stones, there is a loose spongy sward, perhaps not above five or six inches deep, and incapable to produce anything but heath, and all beneath it is hard gravel or rock... Here the workmen first made room to fix their instruments, and then, by strength, and the help of those two mechanic powers, the screw and the lever, they raised out of their ancient beds those massive bodies, and then filling up the cavities with gravel, set them up, mostly end-ways along the sides of the roads, as directions in time of deep snows, being some of them, as they stand, eight or nine feet high. They serve likewise, as memorials of the skill and labour requisite to the performance of so difficult work.

In some particular spots, where there was a proper space beside the stones, the workmen dug hollows, and, by undermining, dropped them in, where they lie buried so securely, as never more to retard the traveller's journey; but it was thought a moot point, even where it was successful, whether any time or labour was saved by this practice; for those pits, for the most part, required to be made very deep and wide, and it could not be foreseen, without continual boring, whether there might not be a rock above the necessary depth, which might be a disappointment after great labour.

The roads on these moors are now as smooth as Constitution Hill, and I have galloped on some of them for miles together in great tranquillity...

When (a) bog has crossed the way on a stony moor, there the loose ground has been dug out down to the gravel, or rock, and the hollow filled up in the manner following, viz.;

First with a layer of large stones, then a smaller size, to fill up the gaps, and raise the causeway higher; and, lastly, two, three or more feet of gravel, to fill up the interstices of the small stones, and form a smooth and binding surface. This part of the road has a bank on each side, to separate it from a ditch, which is made without to receive the water from the bog, and, if the ground will allow it, to convey it by a trench to a slope, and thereby in some measure drain it.

In a rocky way, where no loose stones were to be found, if a bog intervened, and trees could be had at any portable distance, the road has been made solid by timber and fascines, crowned with gravel, dug out from the side of some hill.

This is durable; for the faggots and trees, lying continually in the moisture of the bog, will instead of decaying, become extremely hard, as has been observed of trees that have been plunged into those sloughs, and lain there, in all probability, for many ages. This causeway has likewise a bank and a ditch for the purpose above-mentioned.'

As far as rivers are concerned 'no remedy but bridges has been found... but... how short is human foresight, especially in new projects... The spring of the arch was founded upon rocks, and it was elevated much above the highest water that had ever been known by the country people; yet, some time after it was finished, there happened a sudden torrent from the mountains, which brought down pieces of rocks and trees; and, by its being placed too near the issue of water from between two hills, though firmly built with stone, it was cropt off, not far beneath the crown of the arch, as if it had neither weight not solidity.'

As for declivities, 'the new roads have been carried on in more regular curves than the old paths, and are dug into the hills, which are sloped away above them; and where any rocks have occurred in the performance, they have been bored and blown away with gunpowder.

Above the road are trenches made to receive rains, melting snows, and springs, which last are in many places continually issuing out of the sides of the gills, being drained away from large waters collected in lakes, and other cavities, above, the mountains.

From the above-mentioned trenches are proper channels made to convey the water down the hills; these are secured, by firm pavement, from being gulled by the stream: and in places that required it, there are stone walls built behind the road, to prevent the fall of earth or stones from the broken part of the declivity...

Steep Ascents. As the heights, for the most part are attained, as I have been saying, by going round the sides of the hills from one to another, the exceeding steep ascents are not very common in the ordinary passages: but where they are; inconveniences and difficulties of them have been removed.

I shall only instance in one, which, indeed, is confessed to be the worst of them all. This is the Coriarack mountain, before-mentioned, which rises in the way that leads from Dalwhinny to Fort Augustus. It is above a quarter of a mile of perpendicular height, and was passed by besides the soldiery when the garrisons were changed, as being the nearest way from one of the barracks to the other; and had it not been for the conveniency of that communication, this part of the new roads had never been thought of.

The road over it is carried on upon the south declivity of a hill, by seventeen traverses, like the course of a ship when she is turning to windward, by angles still advancing higher and higher: yet little of it is to be seen below, by reason of flats, hollows, and windings that intercept the sight; and nothing could give you a general view of it, unless one could be supposed to be placed high above the mountain in the air...

Each of the above-mentioned angles is about seventy or eighty yards in length, except in a few places where the hill would not admit of all that extent.

These traverses upward, and the turnings of their extremities, are supported on the outside of the road by stone walls, from ten to fifteen feet in height.

Thus the steep ascent, which was so difficult to be attained, even by the foot passengers, is rendered everywhere more easy for wheel carriages than Highgate-Hill...'

(Burt, ii, pp 192–204)

G: Scale of Equipment for Admission to Hospital

Scale of equipment for soldiers admitted to Edinburgh Royal Infirmary in the middle of the Eighteenth century:

Firelock, Bayonet, Sword or Hanger, Pouch or Shoulder Belt, Waist Belt, Sling, Cartridge Box, Coat, Waistcoat, Breeches, Hatt, Cap, Shirts, Rollers or Stocks, Pairs of Shoes, Pairs of Stockings, Knapsack, Haversack.

(MS305, fol 219v)

H: Barrack and Accommodation Stores, 1747

Proposals by Lieutenant-General Blakeney in 1747 for barrack and accommodation stores for a company of sixty soldiers in Aberdeenshire:

	£	s	d
30 bedsteads at 5s. each	7	10	0
60 pair of Blankets at 6s. each pair	18	0	0
Pot and Pan to each Mess of 6 Men at 6s. each	3	0	0
Salt for the whole of one Season	1	0	0
2 Wooden Bowls to each Mess at 8d. each	0	13	4
2 Dishes of Do. at 6d. each	0	10	0
6 Plates of Do. at 3d. each	0	15	0
10 Water Buckets at 1s. each	0	10	0
10 Pair of Tongs at 1s. each	0	10	0
10 Iron Shovels at 18d. each	0	15	0
10 Coal Boxes or Backets for carrying out the ashes	0	15	0
Supposed they get 10 Tables and 20 Forms from the Fort at Aberdeen	0	0	0
	33	18	4

It was recommended that the 'gentlemen' of the county might consider giving a premium to the soldiers because their sevice was 'fatiguing' and there was a lot of expense for shoes and stockings. Meal, malt, provisions and fuel should be conveyed to the military posts, and charged at the normal county prices. The local landowners should supply wood and give help in building huts. (*Historical Papers, 2, 496-7.*)

The normal scale of bedding for troops appears to have been, per bed, *one* coverlet, *two* pairs of blankets, *two* pairs of sheets, *one* boltster and *one* bed tick. An infantry company comprised seventy-eight men, who, according to the barrack master of Edinburgh Castle, required fortynine beds. After deducting the supernuerary ranks, it would appear that private soldiers must have slept in some form of double bed. Each man had a pair of blankets and a pair of sheets, but two pairs were allotted to each bed, with only one bolster, one coverlet and one bed tick. (*Albemarle Papers, 1, 227.*)

I: The Kingshouses at Dalnacardoch and Dalwhinnie

Dalnacardoch

It is obvious that Dalnacardoch, situated at the junction of the roads from Perth and Stirling to Inverness, occupied a position of importance in the communication system. The soldiers' hut at Dalnamine, about a mile to the south, was taken over as a shealing bothy, but the 'General's Hutt' at Dalnacardoch developed into a Kingshouse, or inn, and continued in this capacity until 1865, when the Duke of Atholl, feeling that the railway had killed road traffic, closed it as an inn.[1] From the Atholl Chronicles it appears that Dalnacardoch first became an inn in 1732, when the Duke of Atholl entered into a contract with Alexander Robertson of Blairfetty, who undertook to build an inn and offices at Dalnacardoch at a cost not exceeding a thousand merks.[2]

During the '45 Dalnacardoch saw quite a lot of military activity. Prince Charles Edward stayed there on his way south in August, 1745, and again, on 10 February, 1746, during the retreat to Inverness. Lord George Murray and his troops were there just a month later, and in the years after Culloden it housed a detachment of Hanoverian troops engaged in patrol work.[3]

The innkeeper in 1757, John McPherson, was obviously unhappy about the condition of his inn, because he wrote to the factor of Lochgarry estates that, 'the House, Stable and Kitchen of Dalnacardich are in very bad repair which gives great Disgust to Travelers, that the Garden Wall is quite down... an Inconvenience to Travellers, as they cannot be accommodated with Roots and Greens.'[4] It was not every innkeeper who was so conscious of the vitamin content of his meals! His complaint was at last recognised in 1759, when there was an estimate for repairs at Dalnacardoch:

'Altering and Mending the Garret floor, putting up 2 partitions and putting in four Sky Lights and plaistering the Walls... 15 bolls lime for harling... New Stair... Total £67 19 4.'[5] The Saga of Dalnacardoch was, however, far from being over. The repairs were carried out, with the inevitable consequence of an increased rent. John McPherson, accordingly, complained on 16 February, 1763, to the Barons of Exchequer in Scotland that he was the 'possessor of the Publick House and farm of Dalnacardich... a mountainous and stormy part of the Highlands... with Winter storms so severe that for the past several years the Houses required to be repaired every Summer... the present rent is as much as the farm can well bear – he has to bring straw and hay from Badenoch and other provendor from Perth – in place of makeing any profit from the Publick House, he has lost considerably by it... his own cattle have died from want of provendor.'[6] The Lords Commissioners of Justiciary reported favourably on the inn, to the effect that they were 'as well accommodate as the said John McPherson could make us.'[7] The factor countered in a report to the Barons of Exchequer that 'this is a stage no Travellers can avoid... expect not only to be well used, but to have things rather in a better and neater way on his Majesty's Grownds than elsewhere... (McPherson) is not the proper landlord... as both he and his wife have never been bred but in the Country way.'[8] The factor went on to point out that as McPherson had done none of things he should have done, repairs would now cost £40 sterling (£480 Scots), adding that he would have to go, unless he agreed to repair the house at his own expense, build an oven in the kitchen and keep a cook.

News of impending changes must have leaked out, because in the following year two applications were received for the inn. The first was from Donald McDonald of Auchtar, who undertook to do all the necessary repairs, claiming that he was young and had a wife 'reared in the low country', thereby subscribing like many others to the snobbish nonsensity that a lowland connection meant efficiency and respectability. The other, John Robertson, described as 'Servant to Sir Adam Fergusson of Kilkerran', quoted in his favour that 'having served in several Families in England he cannot fail to understand keeping a Table better than any person, who by living constantly in the Highlands, has not enjoyed the same advantages.' Robertson obviously subscribed firmly to the Johnsonian dictum that the Scotsman's noblest prospect was the highway leading to London. McDonald was regarded as the lesser, or greater, of two evils and was made the new tacksman on Dalnacardoch, because in 1765, he petitioned Lord George Beauclerk, the Commander in Chief, to the effect that if he were given £25, he would add £25 of his own to carry out repairs.[9] In 1767 McDonald died, but his widow carried on. In applying for renewal of her lease in 1772 she described the roof as being hardly

Plate 1 Marshall Wade, the father of the military roads (*artist unknown*)

Plate 2 The Tay Bridge, Aberfeldy. Wade was justifiably proud of this bridge, designed by William Adam, completed in 1734, and still carrying main road traffic

Plate 3 One of Wade's roads for walkers only today is the track between Moy and Faillie Bridge, close to the proposed realignment of the A9

Plate 4 The Black Rock section of Wade's road by the side of Loch Ness is still in use as a road between Fort Augustus and Inverness

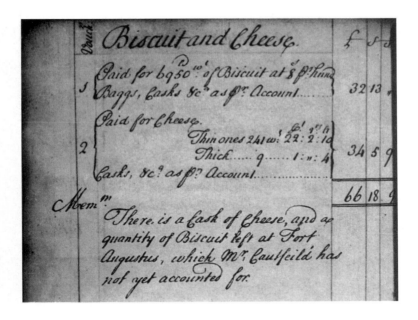

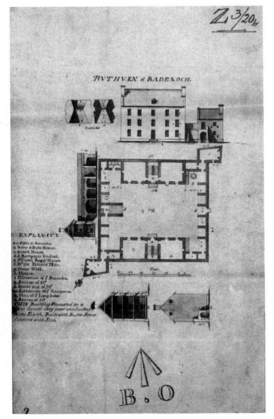

Plate 5 A page from Major Duroure's accounts in General Wade's Letter Book, 1732. Biscuits and cheese were the staple diet of troops on road work

Plate 6 The plan of Ruthven Barracks, an important defence post on the road to Inverness

Plate 7 The former Kingshouse at Garbhamòr on the approach to the Corrieyairack. The building is, unfortunately, being allowed to deteriorate

Plate 8 Corgarff Castle in the wild country at the foot of the Lecht. An existing fortification adapted for military use after the '45

Plate 9 The military road north of Grantown, one of the typical long straight stretches frequently achieved by both Wade and Caulfield presents a striking contrast to Plate 10

Plate 10 The hairpins of the Devil's Staircase. When hills were too steep, the straight line had to be abandoned for a series of traverses

Plate 11 Dulsie Bridge spanning the Findhorn on the road to Fort George is a spectacular bridge

Plate 12 The bridge at Garve on the problematic road from Contin to Poolewe

Plate 13 At the end of a military road, Fort George is a wonderful example of eighteenth–century fortification

Plate 14 A panoramic impression of Glenelg and the Barracks at Bernera, the terminal point of another military road

Plate 15 A fine example of an inscribed marking stone at the Well of the Lecht

Inscription on stone:

A···D1754
FIVE·COMPANES·
FE·33D·REGIMENT·
RIGHT·HONEE·LORD
CHAS·HAY·COLONEL
MADE·FE·ROAD·FROM
HERE·TO·FE
SPEY ≠

Plate 16 The Corse of Slakes: the highest part of the Galloway road looking towards the Cree estuary

waterproof.[10] Two years later the kitchen and brewhouse were burned down, and in the following year Mrs McDonald petitioned for furniture which had been destroyed. meanwhile the Commissioners for the Forfeited Estates, managing Lochgarry estates, appear virtually to have rebuilt Dalnacardoch into a house with ten bedrooms and a garret 'for common travellers and soldiers.'[11] The cost of rebuilding, including harling, was £1200.[12] In 1777 Patrick McNaughton, described as 'vintner in Dalnacardoch' was given an eleven year lease of the inn and the land.

Dalwhinnie

The next Kingshouse on the way north was at Dalwhinnie. In 1784 the Board for the Forfeited Estates took a fifty year lease of the inn at an annual rent of £25.[13] Among the estate papers of Alexander Robertson of Strowan is an insurance policy of the Sun Fire office in London, dated 26 January, 1787, showing that the inn at Dalwhinnie was insured for £400 and the offices for £100.[14] As a footnote, Miss Grant of Rothiemurchus, in her Memoirs, mentioned that in 1820, her butler and cook married, took over the inn at Dalwhinnie, and furnished it out of her lumber room![15]

Notes   1–3 Chronicles of Atholl and Tullibardine.
                 4–10, 13 S.R.O. E 767/12/32/34.
                 11,12,14 Forfeited Estates Papers, 227, 306, 209.
                 15 Grant, 351.

J: Contract for Building Tummel Bridge

'Whereas it is agreed between Lieut Genl George Wade for and on account of His Majesty, and John Stewart of Canagan Esqr, that the said John Stewart shall build a Stone Bridge Strengthened with a double Arch over the River of Tumble, within less than a mile west of the House of the said Canagan, which Bridge is to have an Arch of at least forty two foot between the Landstools /or more if the breadth of the River shall require an Arch of a larger dimension/ It is likewise to be twelve foot in breadth including the Parrapet Walls, which Walls are to be three foot High above the Pavement, and at least one foot broad, and to be Coped with good flag Stones, The whole to be of good materials and well wrought, And to have an Access to the same extending so far on both sides to the Land, as to render it easily passable for Wheel Carriage or Canon, and Likewise to make sufficient Buttments that shall Confine the Water to pass under the Arch, that in extraordinary Floods it may not damage or undermine the foundation, for which Bridge and all Materials, and Charges relating thereto, the said Lieut General George Wade is to pay to the said John Stewart, the Sum of two hundred pounds Sterling Viz: Fifty pounds on the Signing this Contract, and one hundred and fifty Pounds, as soon as the work is completed, which he promises to finish before the last day of October next ensuing, and the said John Stewart does oblige himself to give sufficient Security before the last Payment is made to uphold the said Bridge at his own Expence for the space of twenty Years from the date hereof, whereto we have interchangeably set our hands, this Twenty fifth day of Iuly 1730

Witness John Stewart   (Signed) John Stewart
Witness Donald McDonald'

(S.R.O. GD 1/53/97)

K: The Pre-military Bridges in Dumfries and Galloway

The pre-military bridges between Dumfries and Newton Stewart were:

Bridgend – repaired 1730 (rebuilt 1788)
Courgan – repaired 1728, described as ruinous 1733
Spots Burn – built 1729 (rebuilt 1770)
Bridge of Urr ar Haughford – repaired 1728 (rebuilt 1721)
Graniford Bridge – built 1739
Upper Bridge of Tarff – repaired 1778
Fleet Bridge – built by John Frew in 1729
Glenburn Bridge (Skyreburn) – built 1742, swept away 1745 (rebuilt 1750)
Moneypool Bridge (Creetown) – built 1759, fell 1769 (rebuilt 1770)
Palnure Bridge – repaired 1731 (rebuilt 1740) (one mile above present
                 bridge until 1778)
Cree Bridge – built c 1748 (ninety yards upstream from present bridge)[1]

Alexander Lawrie's estimate for bridges between Dumfries and Port Patrick, 1763

Lochruton Burn and Milnrace Bridges	31	9	0
Milton of Orr Bridge	17	11	2
Spots Burn Bridge	33	11	6
Carlinwark Burn Bridge	9	8	2
Kelton Miln Burn and Milnrace Bridges	23	13	10
Water of Tarff Bridge	64	14	1
Killwhanaty and Rownile Bridges	24	11	1
Auchintalloch Bridge	17	19	3
Skyreburn Bridge	25	2	1
Englishman's Burn Bridge	15	14	4
Middle Burn Bridge	16	15	0
Garrocher Bridge	15	11	9
Monypole Burn Bridge	28	19	5

End of Cree Bridge	28	8	2
Rebuilding of Tarff Bridge	85	5	11
Lady Burn Bridge	20	3	10
Widening and repairng Luce Water Bridge	51	6	6
Balochfargan Burn Bridge	19	0	6
Ballancallantie Burn Bridge	48	0	4
Pallanton Burn Bridge	36	9	6
Two Mile Burn Bridge	16	5	5
	629	18	11[2]

[1] Commissioners of Supply Minutes for the Stewartry of Kirkcudbright, 30 April, 1782.
[2] Arnot, M C, *The Military Road to Port Patrick*, pp 133–4.

Bibliography

Manuscript sources

Much of the material in this book has been based on the following manuscripts: in the National Library of Scotland, General Wade's Letter and Order Book (MS7187), General Bland's Letter and Warrant Books (MS304/5/6), General Churchill's Letter Books (MS307/8/9), and the Letter Book of the Governor of Edinburgh Castle (MS8027); in the Scottish Record Office, the Broughton and Cally Muniments (GD10), the Gordon Castle Collection (GD44), the Stair Papers (GD135), Forfeited Estate Papers (Glengarry and Strowan) (E767), and the Tummel Bridge Document (GD/1/53/97); in the Public Record Office, the King's Warrant Books, War Office Miscellany Book (WO 1), Treasury Minute Books, North Britain Books, Treasury Board Papers, and the Home Office Military Entry Book; in the relevant county offices, the Minutes of the Commissioners of Supply.

Printed sources

Among the most useful of the printed documentary material were the following: *House of Commons Journals, 20–42; Reports of the Commissioners for Highland Roads and Bridges*, 4 vols, 1803–63; *Chronicles of Atholl and Tullibardine*, 5 vols, Edinburgh, 1908; *Culloden Papers*, ed Duff, 1815; *More Culloden Papers*, ed Warrand, 5 vols, 1923–30; *Albemarle Papers*, New Spalding Club, 1902; *Annals of Banff*, New Spalding Club, 1891–3; *Records of the County of Banff 1660–1760*, New Spalding Club, 1922; *Historical Papers Relating to the Jacobite Period 1699–1750*, New Spalding Club, 1895; *Forfeited Estate Papers*, SHS, 1909; *Highland Papers*, 4 vols, SHS, 1914–34; *Collected Papers on the Jacobite Risings*, Jarvis, 2 vols, 1972; *Letters from a Gentleman in the*

North of Scotland, Burt, 2 vols, ed Jamieson, 1822; relevant parishes in the *Old* and *New Statistical Accounts of Scotland*.

Eighteenth-century newspapers and periodicals, such as the *Aberdeen Journal*, *Edinburgh Evening Courant*, *Caledonian Mercury*, and *Scots Magazine* yield useful material, often of a corroborative nature.

There are many good articles in national and local journals and collections, eg: 'Development of the Road System in the Stewartry', Anderson, A. D., *TGDAS*, *44/5*; 'Military Road in Galloway', Arnott, M. C., *TGDAS*, *28*; Bighouse Papers, *TGSI*, *22*; 'The Highland Road Maker & Dashing Red Sergeant', Buist, *Scots Magazine*, *11/12*; 'Military Roads in the Highlands', Mackenzie, *TISS*, *5*; 'Argyllshire Roads Prior to 1800', Mactavish, *TGSI*, *38*; *Commissioners of Supply for the Stewartry*, Maitland, 1933 (reprint from the *Galloway News*); 'General Wade and his Military Roads', Mathieson, *Scottish Geographical Magazine*, *40*; 'Glenelg', Murchison, *TGSI*, *39/40*; 'Edinburgh Castle 1751–3', Rae, *Book of the Old Edinburgh Club*, *32*; 'Old Highland Roads', Ross, *TGSI*, *14*.

Diaries and journals of tours give an interesting, if subjective, background: Boswell's *Journal of a Tour to the Hebrides* (1785), Miss Grant's *Memoirs of a Highland Lady* (1911 edn), Johnson's *Journey to the Western Islands* (1785), Knox's *Tour through the Highlands* (1787), Newte's *Prospects and Observations on a Tour in Scotland* (1785), Pennant's *Tour in Scotland* (4th edn, 1776), Pococke's *Tours in Scotland* (SHS, 1887), Skrine's *Tours in Scotland* (1795), journals of tours by Southey (1929 edn) and Dorothy Wordsworth (1874 edn).

Military road material is to be found in: Salmond, *Wade in Scotland*, Edinburgh, 1938; Bulloch, *Old Highland Highways*, Inverness, 1931; Fraser, *Old Deeside Road*, Aberdeen, 1921; Stephen, 'History of Roads in the Highlands of Scotland' (PhD Thesis of Aberdeen University, 1936); Haldane, *Drove Roads of Scotland*, Edinburgh, 1952, and *New Ways Through the Glens*, Edinburgh, 1962; Donnachie, *Industrial Archaeology of Galloway*, Newton Abbot, 1971.

Cruden, *The Scottish Castle*, 1963, is useful on forts and barracks. Menary, *Duncan Forbes of Culloden*, 1936, Ferguson, *Argyll in the '45*, 1951, and Findlay, *Wolfe in Scotland*, 1928 are useful studies. Mac-William, *A Black Watch Episode of 1731*, Edinburgh, 1908, is short but full of interest.

Moir, *Early Maps of Scotland*, Edinburgh, 1973, and Skelton's short *Military Survey of Scotland*, Edinburgh, 1967, have a wealth of cartographic detail. There is a detailed survey of the road from Braemar to the Spittal of Glenshee by Graham in *Proceedings of the Society of Antiquaries of Scotland, 97*.

The best general history of the period is *Scotland 1689 to the Present* by Ferguson, W., Edinburgh, 1968.

Maps and plans

Maps are the very life's blood of a book of this kind and literally hundreds have been consulted.

In the Map Room of the National Library of Scotland the following are probably the most useful: Roy's Military Survey (photostat); Taylor and Skinner's Survey of 1776; maps of the '45 period by Willdey, Cooper and Rutherford; Stobie's 1783 map of Perthshire; Ainslie's maps of Wigtown (1789) and the Stewartry (1797); Crawford's map of Dumfriesshire (1804), and all the Ordnance Survey six-inch maps.

In the manuscript section are plans of most of the forts and barracks in the 'Z' series, also Morrison's 1749 survey of the military road from Loch Lubnaig to Glen Ogle (Z 3/39a).

In the Scottish Record Office, among the Stair Papers, maps RHP 2741/1/2/3 are all of the Stranraer/Ballantrae area.

The Royal Scottish Geographical Society has a photostat 'Wade Collection' including the proposed Glen Feshie road.

The Public Record Office has surveys 'Fort George to Bellamoor' n.d., MPHH36; Blairgowrie to Braemar 1750, MPH14; Glenogle to Crianlarich, 1750, and Glenogle to Blackmount, 1751, MR479.

In the Map Room of the British Museum are the originals of Roy's Military Survey; survey Fort William to Kinlochleven 1748, 1750, P56/5261; and in the series 'Royal XLVIII' the following surveys: Dumbarton to Inveraray 1745 (59), Fort Augustus to Bernera (60b, 62, 63), Stirling to Amulree (64), Corgarff to Braemar (73, 74), Dulsie Bridge to Forres and Nairn (71), River Findhorn to River Avon (69), River Avon to Braemar (68), Blairgowrie to Braemar (Morrison 1750) (67).

Acknowledgements

I should like to record my grateful thanks to the many people who have helped in the making of this book and who, alas, are too numerous to name individually. Nevertheless some names must appear: Mr A. D. Anderson of Maxwelltown, who put his unrivalled knowledge of the Stewartry roads at my disposal and for drawing to my attentions a book published in 1993–Robertson, J., *The Public Roads and Bridges in Dumfrieshire 1650–1820*, Cromwell Press; all those who have found it no trouble to put national and local records at my disposal; groups of my students who have helped with practical surveys; my colleagues, especially Mr A. W. Harding, in the History Department of Dundee College of Education; Lt-Col I. B. Cameron Taylor, formerly of the National Trust for Scotland, who in the early stages helped to turn castles in Spain into a reality.

It would be an act of gross ingratitude not to acknowledge the help of my sons, Iain and David, who accompanied me on so many of the walks on the military roads and whose youthful limbs saved me from mony a weary trauchle.

Finally my most grateful thanks are due to my wife, who has several times read every work with a kindly and critical eye, and without whose help in so many ways this book would never have seen the light of day.

Thanks are also due to following for the loan of illustrations and for permission to reproduce them: *Aberdeen Journals*, plates 8, 11; Dr James Bruce, Plate 12; John Dewar Studios, plate 13; the National Library of Scotland, plates 5, 6, 14; and the Society of Antiquaries of Scotland, plate 1, The remaining plates are from the author's collection.

Maps 2–34 based on Ordnance Survey One Inch maps with the sanction of the Controller of HM Stationery Office; Crown copyright reserved.

Glossary

bait	refreshment
carriage	any wheeled vehicle
Commissioners of Supply	a committee of landowners, each possessing at least £100 (Scots) annual rent, fulfilling some of the functions of a county council from the seventeenth century to 1888
country	local district or area; 'county'
coup	tilt
crow	crowbar
deals	planks
fiars prices	standard and legal price of grain for each county, fixed by the sheriff, advised by a jury of landowners
furth	out of the country, abroad
gavelock	crowbar, lever
harling	rough-cast
heritor	landowner in a parish, liable for public burdens
mash	stonebreaking hammer
mell	wooden hammer or mallet
ploughgate	a fiscal unit represented by approximately 104 acres of arable
sway	a small hand crane
yr	younger, as in a title

Index

(References to illustrations are in italic type)

203

Statute labour, 13, 64, 89, 93, 101, 113, 121, 173; supplementary tax 93, 97, 120
Stirling Castle, 21, 36, 72
Stone, Galloway and Linlithgow, 106
Sutlers, 41

Tar, 39
Telford, Thomas, 37, 53, 74, 89, 90, 117, 124, 126–7
Tents, 42, 67, 73, 79, 84
Timber haulage, 38, 77
Tools, 35, 37, 64, 90, 94
Trapeaud, Governor, 84
Traverses, 39, 56, 68, 127, 147, 162

Turnpike Trustees, Perthshire, 67–8

Wade, General, *185*; 1724 Report on Highlands, 18; C-in-C, North Britain, 18; 1726 Report on Highlands, 46; 1727 Memorial, 46; promoted Lt-Gen, 21; promoted General, 23; promoted Field Marshal, 23; did, 23; road mileage, 60; stone, 137
Watson, Col David, 30, 35, 77, 97
West Highlands Railway, 74
Working parties, *see* Road making